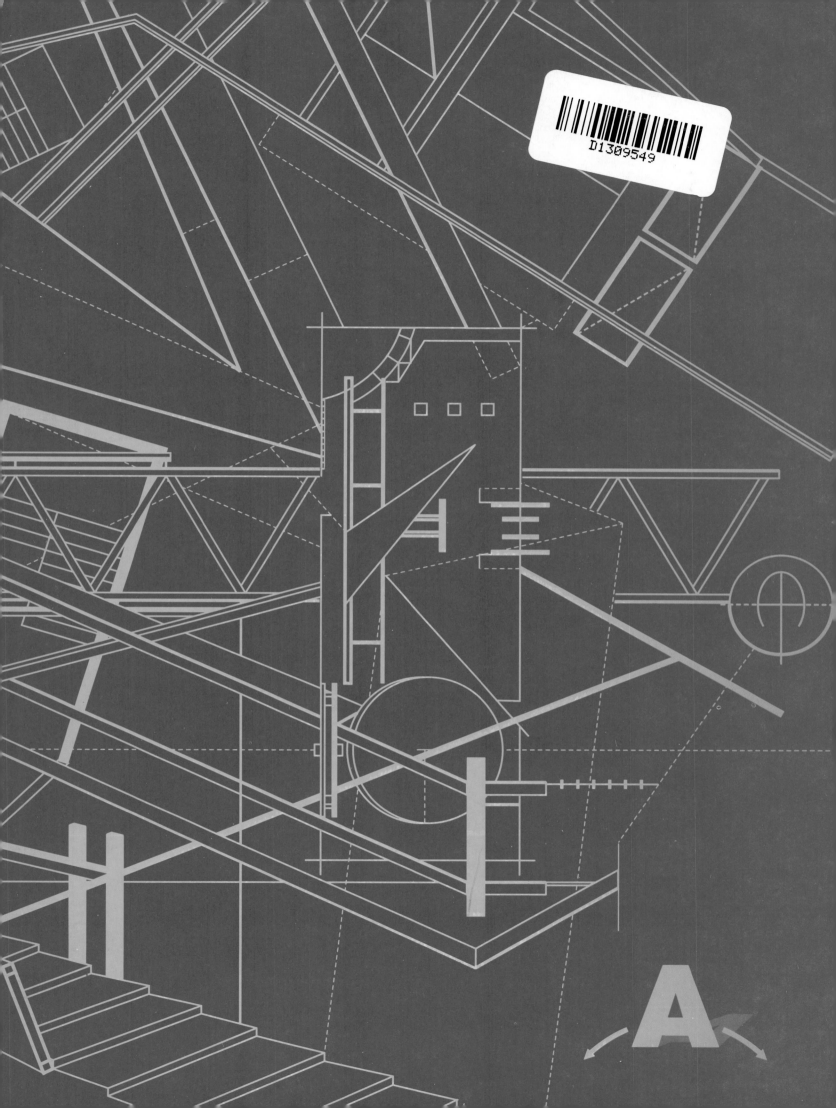

The

American

Directory

of

Architects

SOUTH/SOUTHEAST

Creative Director / President: **JOEL FULLER** *Publisher:* **PHILIP SMITH** *Managing Partner:* **PATRICK FIORENTINO**

Art Director / Vice President: **MARK CANTOR** *Art Director / Designer:* **TOM STERLING** *Editor / Marketing Director:*

LAURIE BIEDRZYCKI *Production Director:* **HERK HERNANDEZ** *Production Assistants:* **SUZETTE SULLIVAN**

AND LAURA SCHALLER *Type Designer / Computer Illustrations:* **RALF SCHUETZ** *Accounting:* **SUSAN LATHAM**

ELECTRONIC, MECHANICAL, PHOTOCOPYING, RECORDING OR OTHERWISE, WITHOUT PRIOR PERMISSION OF THE PUBLISHER. PUBLISHED BY PINKHAUS PUBLICATIONS, 2424 SOUTH DIXIE HIGHWAY, MIAMI, FLORIDA 33133, (305) 854-1000. DISTRIBUTED BY ARRANGEMENT WITH ALLWORTH PRESS, 10 EAST 23RD STREET, NEW YORK, NEW YORK 10010. DISTRIBUTOR TO THE TRADE IN THE UNITED STATES: CONSORTIUM BOOK SALES & DISTRIBUTION, INC., 287 EAST 6TH STREET, SUITE 365, SAINT PAUL, MINNESOTA 55101. WORLDWIDE DISTRIBUTION BY HEARST BOOKS INTERNATIONAL, 105 MADISON AVENUE, NEW YORK, NEW YORK 10016. THE AMERICAN DIRECTORY OF ARCHITECTS (ISBN 0-9628934-0-4) ©1991 PINKHAUS PUBLICATIONS INC. PRINTED BY EVERBEST PRINTING COMPANY, LTD, HONG KONG, THROUGH FOUR COLOUR IMPORTS LTD, LOUISVILLE.

Photographic Artwork: **JAMES PALMA** *Special thanks to all participating architects for their generous and patient support of this publication*

Contents

Introduction

In this volume, the American Directory of Architects presents exceptional examples of recent architecture built in the south and southeast. Both local and national architects have come to imprint the region with their particular vision. Expansive opportunities for stylistic experimentation combined with an inviting environment have fostered the area's explosive architectural growth. Nationwide, architects have been influenced by the design renaissance that began in the south. Under the southern sun, hybrid architectural styles blossomed like hothouse flowers. More often than not, select characteristics of post-modernism combined and interacted with indigenous architectural elements to produce a unique regional style. In Texas, for example, the rich hues of the clay soil and Pueblo buildings can be seen in the architectural palette. Throughout Florida, the lush sweetness of tropical flora has enveloped atriums, facades and even the overall concept of residential developments. Georgia and Louisiana have drawn on their historic architectural legacy producing a traditional elegance tempered by a southern sensibility. 🏮 Collected here for the first time, is a pictorial survey of the varied and broad scope of the region's building. The office towers, museums, country clubs, hotels, civic centers, historic restorations, stadiums, universities and private residences published here all have their impact on the contemporary architectural landscape. Projects featured range from the whimsical Walt Disney World Swan Hotel by Michael Graves, the classical Dade County Cultural Center by John Burgee to the Spanish-Mediterranean private villas by Pandula Architects. Whether you are an architect, a developer, residential client or historian, this publication serves as an invaluable sourcebook of outstanding architectural firms.

Architects

ADACHE ASSOCIATES, ARCHITECTS, PA

550 S. Federal Highway
Ft. Lauderdale, FL 33301

305 525 8133

FIRM SPECIALTY:

Hotels / Resorts

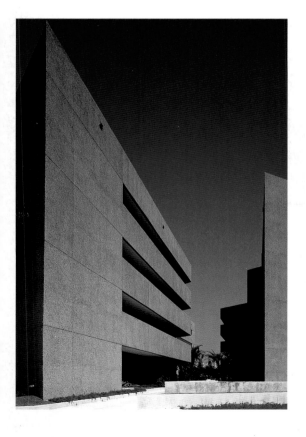

TOP
Art Institute of
Ft. Lauderdale
Ft. Lauderdale, FL
Photo: Joe Wagstaff

CENTER
The Sunrise Inn, 1990
Ft. Lauderdale. FL
Photo: Andrew Rubenstein

BOTTOM LEFT
One University Drive
Plantation, FL
Photo: Linda Meers

BOTTOM RIGHT
Port de Plaisance, 1990
St. Maarten, N.A.

P. O. Box 165036

Miami, FL 33116

305 670 0477

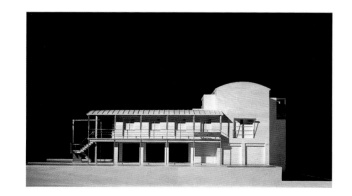

THIS **P**AGE

Key-Haus

Florida Keys, FL

Photos: Raul Pedroso

Model & Drawing:

E. Castiñeira

GIORGIO BALLI ARCHITECT, AIA

9835 Sunset Drive

Suite 209

Miami, FL 33173

305 595 6595

FIRM SPECIALTY:

Residential

TOP
Residence, 1984
Coral Gables, FL
Photo: Kurt Waldmann

CENTER
Residence, 1982
Coral Gables, FL
Photo: Kurt Waldmann

BOTTOM LEFT
Small Office Building
South Miami, FL
Photo: George Miller

BOTTOM RIGHT
Residence, 1984
Coral Gables, FL
Photo: Kurt Waldmann

TOP
School of Business
Administration
University of Miami
Coral Gables, FL

BOTTOM
School of Business
Administration
University of Miami
Coral Gables, FL

TOP RIGHT
Florida City
Elementary School
Florida City, FL

CENTER RIGHT
School of Business
Administration
University of Miami
Coral Gables, FL

BOTTOM RIGHT
Rickenbacker Causeway
Toll Facility,
Miami, FL
Photos: Deborah Young

4649 Ponce de Leon Blvd.
Suite 402
Coral Gables, FL 33146
305 667 3109

LEFT
NCNB Center &
Pennzoil Place
Houston, TX

TOP RIGHT
Atlantic Center
Atlanta, GA

CENTER RIGHT
Dade County
Cultural Center
Miami, FL

BOTTOM RIGHT
Transco Tower
Houston, TX
Photos: Richard Payne

885 Third Avenue
New York, NY 10022
212 751 7440

BENJAMIN P. BUTERA, AIA

815 Orienta Avenue
Suite 1005
Altamonte Springs,
FL 32701
407 332 6650

FIRM SPECIALTY:
Custom, Commercial and
Residential Architecture

TOP
Stockman Residence, 1990
Ormond Beach, FL
Photo: Michael Lowery

CENTER
Culbreth Residence, 1988
Daytona Beach, FL
Photo: Peter Burgh

BOTTOM LEFT
Burger King Administration
Building, 1987
Daytona Beach, FL
Photo: Ben Butera

BOTTOM RIGHT
Buswell-Charkow
Residence, 1989
Windermere, FL
Photo: Michael Lowery

CAMPBELL POPE & ASSOCIATES, INC.

3390 Peachtree Road

Suite 1046

Atlanta, GA 30326

404 233 6847

THIS PAGE

Pavé Villa Retail

Jewelry Store

Augusta Mall

Augusta, GA

Photos: Robert Wells

CHRIS CONSULTANTS INC.

1520 W. Airport Freeway
Irving, TX 75062
214 253 3583

FIRM SPECIALTY:

Private Clubs

TOP
Gleneagles Country Club
Dallas, TX
Photo: C. Nieman

CENTER
Corpus Christi Town Club
Corpus Christi, TX
Photo: R.O. Bumpass

BOTTOM LEFT
Prestonwood
Country Club, 1989
Cary, NC

BOTTOM RIGHT
Gleneagles Country Club
Entry Foyer
Dallas, TX
Photo: R.O. Bumpass

25 Seabreeze Avenue
Delray Beach, FL 33483
407 276 4951

FIRM SPECIALTY:
Architecture / Planning /
Interior Design

TOP
Newport Bay Clubhouse
Boca Raton, FL
Photo: Fred Leavitt

CENTER
25 Seabreeze
Office Building
Delray Beach, FL
Photo: Dan Forer

BOTTOM LEFT
Interstate Centre
Ft. Lauderdale, FL
Photo: Dan Forer

BOTTOM RIGHT
Temple Sinai
Delray Beach, FL
Photo: Dan Forer

DALTON MORAN SHOOK ARCHITECTURE, INC.

114-1/2 West Fifth Street

Charlotte, NC 28202

704 372 0116

FAR LEFT, TOP
Wayne Towne Center
Wayne, NJ
Photo: Mitchell Kearney

FAR LEFT, BOTTOM
Food Court at Myrtle
Square Mall
Myrtle Beach, SC
Photo: Tim Buchman

FAR LEFT
McMullen Creek
Charlotte, NC
Photo: Tim Buchman

TOP
Schaefer Systems
International
Charlotte, NC
Photo: Tim Buchman

BOTTOM LEFT
North Carolina Federal
Charlotte, NC
Photo: Tim Buchman

BOTTOM RIGHT
Wayne Towne Center
Wayne, NJ
Photo: Mitchell Kearney

LUCY CAROL DAVIS ASSOCIATES

976 Airport Road
Suite 200
Chapel Hill, NC 27514
919 933 7775

TOP
Office Building for
Cornerstone
Associates, 1991
Chapel Hill, NC
Photo: Steven A. Fisher

CENTER
Builders' Showcase
Home, 1989
Charlotte, NC
Photo: Gordon H.
Schenck, Jr.

BOTTOM LEFT
Private Residence, 1990
Chapel Hill, NC
Photo: Steven A. Fisher

BOTTOM RIGHT
Orange County Public
Works Administration
Building, 1989
Hillsborough, NC
Photo: Jerry Markatos

DIEDRICH ARCHITECTS & ASSOCIATES

3399 Peachtree Road
Suite 820
Atlanta, GA 30326
404 364 9633

FIRM SPECIALTY:
Golf Clubhouses

TOP
Admirals Cove
Clubhouse, 1988
Jupiter, FL
Photo: Alan McGee

CENTER
Country Club of the
South, 1988
Atlanta, GA
Photo: John Wadsworth

BOTTOM LEFT
Grand Cypress Golf
Clubhouse
Orlando, FL
Photo: Gabriel Benzur

BOTTOM RIGHT
Wynstone Golf
Clubhouse, 1989
North Barrington, IL
Photo: Hedrich Blessing

DAN C. DUCKHAM, ARCHITECT

3197 N.E. 18th Terrace

Ft. Lauderdale, FL 33306

305 564 5730

and Cashiers, NC

FIRM SPECIALTY:
Architecture/Interior
Design, Residential &
Commercial

FAR LEFT, TOP
Residence, 1989
Ft. Lauderdale, FL
Photo: William H. Sanders

FAR LEFT, BOTTOM
Reed Residence, 1964
Coral Springs, FL
Photo: Wade Swicord

FAR LEFT
Pete's Restaurant &
Lounge, 1988
Boca Raton, FL
Photo: William H. Sanders

TOP
Residence, 1990
Hollywood, FL
Photo: William H. Sanders

BOTTOM LEFT
Pete's Restaurant &
Lounge, 1988
Boca Raton, FL
Photo: William H. Sanders

BOTTOM RIGHT
Unicorn Village
Restaurant, 1990
North Miami Beach, FL
Photo: William H. Sanders

125 N. Robertson Blvd.
Los Angeles, CA 90048
213 278 1915

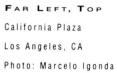

FAR LEFT, TOP
California Plaza
Los Angeles, CA
Photo: Marcelo Igonda

FAR LEFT, BOTTOM
Museum of Anthropology
University of British
Columbia, Vancouver, B.C
Photo: Arthur Erickson
Architects

FAR LEFT
Robson Square Law
Courts
Vancouver B.C.
Photo: Ezra Stoller

TOP
San Diego
Convention Center
San Diego, CA
Photo: Peter Aaron-Esto
Photographics

BOTTOM LEFT
Roy Thomson Hall
Toronto, Canada
Photo: Fiona Spalding-
Smith

BOTTOM RIGHT
Canadian Chancery
Washington, DC
Photo: Paul Warchol

FILER AND HAMMOND ARCHITECTS, INC.

250 Catalonia Avenue
Suite 805
Coral Gables, FL 33134
305 444 5714

FIRM SPECIALTY:
Commercial, Residential &
Institutional

TOP
Estevez Residence
Coral Gables, FL
Photo: Raul Pedroso

CENTER
Estevez Residence
Coral Gables, FL
Photo: Raul Pedroso

BOTTOM LEFT
Biltmore II
Coral Gables, FL
Photo: Kurt Waldmann

BOTTOM RIGHT
Biltmore II, Atrium
Coral Gables, FL
Photo: Kurt Waldmann

GIBSON & SILKWORTH ARCHITECTS & ASSOCIATES, INC.

606 Azalea Lane
Vero Beach, FL 32963
407 231 6008

FIRM SPECIALTY:
Custom Residential

TOP
Private Residence
John's Island, FL

CENTER
Private Residence
John's Island, FL

BOTTOM LEFT
Island Residence
John's Island, FL

BOTTOM RIGHT
Ocean Place
John's Island, FL
Photos: Kim Sargent

341 Nassau Street
Princeton, NJ 08540
609 924 6409

FAR LEFT
Walt Disney World
Swan Hotel
Lake Buena Vista, FL
Photo: William Taylor

TOP
Walt Disney World
Dolphin Hotel
Lake Buena Vista, FL
Photo: William Taylor

BOTTOM LEFT
Michael C. Carlos Hall
Emory University
Egyptian Gallery
Atlanta, GA
Photo: Paschall/Taylor

BOTTOM RIGHT
Michael C. Carlos Hall
Emory University
Entrance Rotunda
Atlanta, GA
Photo: Paschall/Taylor

4217 Ponce de Leon Blvd.
Coral Gables, FL 33146
305 441 0888

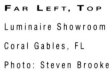

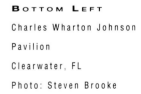

FAR LEFT, TOP
Luminaire Showroom
Coral Gables, FL
Photo: Steven Brooke

FAR LEFT, BOTTOM
Turner Guilford Knight
Correctional Center
Dade County, FL
Photo: Raul Pedroso

FAR LEFT
Tokyo Rose Restaurant
North Miami, FL
Photo: Carlos Domenech

TOP
U.S. Coast Guard Facility
Miami Beach, FL
Photo: Raul Pedroso

BOTTOM LEFT
Charles Wharton Johnson
Pavilion
Clearwater, FL
Photo: Steven Brooke

BOTTOM RIGHT
Mateu Residence
Dade County, FL
Photo: Carlos Domenech

HELLMUTH, OBATA & KASSABAUM, INC.

St. Louis, MO
314 421 2000

Dallas, TX
214 739 6688

Tampa, FL
813 281 0533

FAR LEFT, TOP
Burger King Corporation
World Headquarters
Miami, FL

FAR LEFT, BOTTOM
Burger King Corporation
World Headquarters
Miami, FL

FAR LEFT
AmSouth-Harbert Plaza
Birmingham, AL

TOP
Orange County
Convention & Civic Center
Orlando, FL

BOTTOM LEFT
The Galleria
Dallas, TX
Photos: George Cott

BOTTOM RIGHT
Collin County
Community College
Spring Creek Campus
Plano, TX
Photo: Blackmon Winters

INSPACE/WHITENER-ROHE, INC.

1201 Griffin Street West
Dallas, TX 75215
214 428 8080

FIRM SPECIALTY:
Architecture/Interiors/
Construction

TOP
Stone Canyon Residence
Dallas, TX
Photo: J. Rohe

CENTER
Houshang Gallery, S.F.
Sante Fe, NM
Photo: D. Marlow

BOTTOM LEFT
Hegi Weekend Retreat
Cedar Creek Lake, TX
Photo: Jim Fox

BOTTOM RIGHT
Stone Canyon Residence
Dallas, TX
Photo: J. Rohe

1130 Quintard Avenue
Anniston, AL 36201
205 237 1607

FIRM SPECIALTY:
Interior Architecture

THIS PAGE
College of
Communications, 1990
Jacksonville State
University
Jacksonville, AL
Photo: Tommy L.
Thompson

111 West 57th Street
New York, NY 10019

212 977 6500

FIRM SPECIALTY:

Commercial

FAR LEFT, TOP
Interstate Tower
Charlotte, NC
Photo: Gordon Schenck

FAR LEFT, BOTTOM
World Bank
Under Construction
Washington, DC
Photo: Jock Pottle

FAR LEFT
Third National Bank
Nashville, TN
Photo: Jock Pottle

TOP
Federal Reserve Bank
of Dallas
Under Construction
Dallas, TX
Photo: Jock Pottle

BOTTOM LEFT
Franklin Court
Under Construction
Washington, DC
Photo: Jock Pottle

BOTTOM RIGHT
U.S. International
Trade Commission
Washington, DC
Photo: Steve Gottlieb

MAGILL ARCHITECTS, INC.

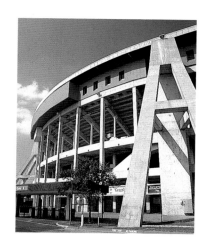

11615 Forest Central Dr.

Suite 211

Dallas, TX 75243

214 343 1981

FIRM SPECIALTY:

Sports / Restoration /

Retail / Interiors

FAR LEFT

Rusk Building

Stephen F. Austin

State University

Nacogdoches, TX

Photo: James B.

Cloutman, III

TOP

Walnut Hill

Office Building

Las Colinas, TX

Photo: James B.

Cloutman, III

BOTTOM LEFT

Units, 1990

Nashville, TN

Photo: Bill LaFevor

BOTTOM RIGHT

Texas Stadium

Irving, TX

Photo: James B.

Cloutman, III

1055 St. Charles Avenue
Suite 402
New Orleans, LA 70130
504 586 1870

FIRM SPECIALTY:
Architecture
Historic Restoration
Museum Planning

FAR LEFT, TOP
Old United States Mint
Restoration: Louisiana
State Museum, 1980
New Orleans, LA
Photo: Alan Karchmer
Original Architect:
William Strickland

FAR LEFT, BOTTOM
Old Louisiana State
Capitol Restoration:
Louisiana State
Museum, 1987
Baton Rouge, LA
Photo: David Gleason
Original Architect:
James H. Dakin

TOP
Benjamin Franklin High
School, 1990
New Orleans, LA
Photo: Alan Karchmer

BOTTOM LEFT
Louisiana Nature and
Science Center, 1980
New Orleans, LA
Photo: Alan Karchmer

BOTTOM RIGHT
Weinstein's Clothing
Store, 1985
New Orleans, LA
Photo: Alan Karchmer

220 East Forsyth Street
Jacksonville, FL 32202
904 356 4195

FAR LEFT
Oceanfront
Condominium, 1975
Ocean City, MD
Photo: Bob Lautman

TOP
Bloomingdales, 1984
Miami, FL
Photo: Steven Brooke

BOTTOM LEFT
Morgan Residence, 1974
Atlantic Beach, FL
Photo: W. Morgan

BOTTOM RIGHT
Westinghouse
World Headquarters,
Steam-Turbine
Division, 1984
Orlando, FL
Photo: Steven Brooke

265 Court Avenue
Memphis, TN 38103
901 525 5344

FIRM SPECIALTY:
Architecture
Interior Design
Planning

TOP
Crescent Center Office
Complex, 1986
Memphis, TN
Photo: Allen Mims

CENTER
Marriott Hotel, 1986
Huntsville, AL
Photo: Allen Mims

BOTTOM LEFT
Slumber Products
Manufacturing/Office
Facility, 1979
Memphis, TN
Photo: Alan Karchmer

BOTTOM RIGHT
Center for Agricultural
Research and Public
Service, 1989
Jackson, TN
Photo: Craig Baird

THE NICHOLS PARTNERSHIP, INC.

2600 Douglas Road
Coral Gables, FL 33134
305 443 5206

FIRM SPECIALTY:
Hotel/Resort
Mixed-use Centers

TOP
The Alhambra, 1987
Coral Gables, FL
Photo: Carlos Domenech

BOTTOM LEFT
Grand Bay Hotel, 1984
Coconut Grove, FL
Photo: Dan Forer

BOTTOM RIGHT
Design Center of the
Americas, 1986
Dania, FL
Photo: Dan Forer

225 Southern Blvd.

Suite 201

W. Palm Beach, FL 33405

407 832 3614

FIRM SPECIALTY:

Custom Residential &

Corporate Offices

FAR LEFT, TOP
Renovations to a small
Residence
West Palm Beach, FL

FAR LEFT, BOTTOM
Renovations to a small
Residence
West Palm Beach, FL

TOP
Private Residence, 1989
West Palm Beach, FL

BOTTOM LEFT
Private Residence,
Pool/Cabana
West Palm Beach, FL

BOTTOM RIGHT
Private Residence, Detail
West Palm Beach, FL
Photos: Kim Sargent

222 Altara

Coral Gables, FL 33146

305 446 1700

FIRM SPECIALTY:

Tropical Architecture

FAR LEFT
Office of Charles
Harrison Pawley, 1990
Coral Gables, FL
Photo: Dan Forer

TOP
Goihman Residence, 1980
Miami Beach, FL
Photo: Martin Fine

BOTTOM LEFT
Caribbean
Marketplace, 1990
"Little Haiti", Miami, FL
Photo: Dan Forer

BOTTOM RIGHT
Smith Residence, 1985
Coconut Grove, FL

LEFT

Morton H. Myerson
Symphony Center
Dallas, TX
Photo: Paul Warchol

TOP RIGHT

First Interstate Bank
Tower, 1986
Dallas, TX
Photo: Wes Thompson

CENTER RIGHT

Morton H. Myerson
Symphony Center
Dallas, TX
Photo: Nathaniel
Lieberman

BOTTOM RIGHT

Centrust Building
Miami, FL, 1986
Photo: Nathaniel
Lieberman

600 Madison Avenue
New York, NY 10022
212 751 3122

6251 Chancellor Drive
Suite 100
Orlando, FL 32809
407 857 5964

FIRM SPECIALTY:
Landscape Architecture
and Planning

FAR LEFT, TOP
Mizner Tower
Boca Raton, FL

FAR LEFT, BOTTOM
Ritz-Carlton Hotel
Naples, FL

FAR LEFT
Ritz-Carlton Hotel
Naples, FL

TOP
The Disney-MGM Studios
Theme Park at Walt
Disney World Resort, FL

BOTTOM LEFT
The Disney Grand
Floridian Hotel at The
Walt Disney World
Resort, FL

BOTTOM RIGHT
Laguna Springs
Ft. Lauderdale, FL
Photos: Art Becker

PORTMAN FRUCHTMAN VINSON ARCHITECTS, INC.

1700 Water Place
Suite 200
Atlanta, GA 30339
404 859 0323

FIRM SPECIALTY:
Hospitality, Commercial,
Medical, Residential

FAR LEFT
The Plimsoll Hotel
Savannah, GA
Artist: C.T. Vinson

TOP
Lakeside Office Building
Peachtree City, GA
Artist: Dan Harmon Assoc.

BOTTOM LEFT
Seapointe Hotel
Wildwood Crest, NJ
Artist: C.T. Vinson

BOTTOM RIGHT
MacDonald Residence
Atlanta, GA
Artist: C.T. Vinson

225 Peachtree Street
Suite 200
Atlanta, GA 30303
404 522 8811

FAR LEFT, TOP
Northpark 500, 1989
Atlanta, GA
Photo: Michael Portman

FAR LEFT, BOTTOM
R. Howard Dobbs
University Center, 1986
Atlanta, GA
Photo: Timothy Hursley

FAR LEFT
One Peachtree Center, 1992
Atlanta, GA
Photo: Gabriel Benzur

TOP
Rockefeller Center
Renovation, 1985
New York, NY
Photo: Jaime Ardiles-Arce

BOTTOM LEFT
Pan Pacific Hotel, 1987
San Francisco, CA
Photo: Jaime Ardiles-Arce

BOTTOM RIGHT
Atlanta Marriott
Marquis, 1985
Atlanta, GA
Photo: Jaime Ardiles-Arce

Calle Sojo, El Rosal
Caracas, Venezuela

33 05 89

TOP

Soto Grande Apartment
Building, 1988
Caracas, Venezuela
Photo: Alberto Rivas-Kerdel

BOTTOM LEFT

Banco Mercantil, 1990
Barcelona, Venezuela
Photo: Maria L. Dias-Aidos

BOTTOM RIGHT

Leary House, 1985
Coconut Grove, FL
Photo: Steven Brooke

7600 Burnet Road

Austin, TX 78757

512 452 6744

FIRM SPECIALTY:

Commercial Interior

Architecture

THIS PAGE

Bookstop-Sunset

Ridge, 1989

San Antonio, TX

Photo: R. Greg Hursley

RTKL ASSOCIATES INC.

One East Broward Blvd.
Suite 303
Ft. Lauderdale, FL 33301
305 764 0500

FAR LEFT, TOP
Esperanté, 1989
West Palm Beach, FL
Photo: Scott McDonald/
Hedrich-Blessing

FAR LEFT, BOTTOM
Hyatt Regency Grand
Cayman, 1986
Grand Cayman Island
Photo: Rion Rizzo

FAR LEFT
Esperanté, 1989
West Palm Beach, FL
Photo: Scott McDonald/
Hedrich-Blessing

TOP
Hyatt Regency Grand
Cayman, 1986
Grand Cayman Island
Photo: Rion Rizzo

BOTTOM LEFT
Burdines, 1986
Palm Beach Gardens, FL
Photo: Tom Knibbs

BOTTOM RIGHT
Strawbridge & Clothier
King of Prussia, PA
Photo: Matt Wargo

SASAKI ASSOCIATES, INC.

64 Pleasant Street
Watertown, MA 02172
617 926 3300

FIRM SPECIALTY:
Multidisciplinary Services

FAR LEFT, TOP
The Village Center
The Landings
Skidaway Island, GA
Photo: Gabriel Benzur

FAR LEFT, BOTTOM
Harbourtown, Sea Pines
Plantation
Hilton Head Island, SC
Photo: Alan Ward

FAR LEFT
Cypress Park
Coral Springs, FL
Photo: Sasaki Associates

TOP
St. Petersburg Pier
St. Petersburg, FL
Photo: Tori Butt

BOTTOM LEFT
Radisson Hotel
Merchandise Mart
Miami Beach, FL
Photo: Tori Butt

BOTTOM RIGHT
The Vineyards
Golf Clubhouse
Naples, FL
Photo: Tori Butt

SISKIND-CARLSON & PARTNERS

528 Waterfront
NW 7th Avenue
Miami, FL 33136
305 547 1333

FIRM SPECIALTY:
Planning, Residential,
Commercial & Resort
Design

TOP
Nestlé Headquarters
(Corporate)
Purchase, NY
Photo: Andrew Gordon

CENTER
Commodore Island Condos
Toledo, OH
Photo: Mark Oburst

BOTTOM LEFT
Ives Corporate Center
North Miami, FL
Photo: Carlos Domenech

BOTTOM RIGHT
South Ferry Plaza
Competition
New York, NY
Artist: Howard Associates

SMALLWOOD, REYNOLDS, STEWART, STEWART & ASSOCIATES, INC.

One Piedmont Center

Suite 303

Atlanta, GA 30305

404 233 5453

100 South Ashley Drive

Suite 1670

Tampa, FL 33602

813 221 1226

FIRM SPECIALTY:

Architecture

Interior Design

Landscape Architecture

TOP

Federal Home Loan

Bank Building

Atlanta, GA

Photo: Gabriel Benzur

CENTER

C & S Plaza

Executive Offices

Columbia, SC

Photo: Jon Miller

BOTTOM LEFT

C & S Plaza

Columbia, SC

Photo: Chris Hamilton

BOTTOM RIGHT

C & S Plaza

Banking Lobby

Columbia, SC

Photo: Jon Miller

BARRY SUGERMAN, ARCHITECT PA AIA

12601 NE 7th Avenue
North Miami, FL 33161
305 893 6055

FIRM SPECIALTY:
Custom Residence

FAR LEFT
Weiner Residence
North Miami, FL
Photo: Tom Knibbs

TOP
Krieger Residence
South Miami, FL
Photo: Mark Surloff

BOTTOM LEFT
Messick Residence
Big Sky, MT
Photo: Dan Forer

BOTTOM RIGHT
Sochet Residence
Islamorada, Florida Keys
Photo: Bob Stein

TOP

McDonnell Douglas Space
Systems Building
Titusville, FL
Photo: Rusty Flynn

BOTTOM

Pensacola Civic Center
Pensacola, FL
Photo: Doug McKay

TOP **R**IGHT

Knoll International
Dallas, TX
Photo: Art Beaulieu

CENTER **R**IGHT

Union Electric Company
Headquarters
St. Louis, MO
Photo: Tony Carosella

BOTTOM **R**IGHT

Criminal Justice Center
Nashville, TN
Photo: Tony Carosella

1900 Summit Tower Blvd.
Suite 300
Orlando, FL 32810
407 875 0222

St. Louis, MO
Washington, DC
Dallas, TX

SWANKE HAYDEN CONNELL ARCHITECTS

1221 Brickell Avenue
Suite 1560
Miami, FL 33131
305 536 8600

FIRM SPECIALTY:
Architecture
Interior Design

FAR LEFT
Del Monte Headquarters
Coral Gables, FL
Photo: Dan Forer

TOP
Southeast Bank
Miami, FL
Photo: Nancy Watson

BOTTOM LEFT
SHCA Offices
Miami, FL
Photo: Nancy Watson

BOTTOM RIGHT
1401 Brickell Avenue
Miami, FL
Artist: Perspectives

1111 Lincoln Road
Suite 300
Miami Beach, FL 33139
305 673 6002

FIRM SPECIALTY:
High-rise Residential/
Single Family
Development

FAR LEFT
Valencia
Boca Raton, FL
Photo: Gary Doty

TOP
Turnberry Isle Yacht &
Racquet Club
Aventura, FL
Photo: Robert M. Swedroe

BOTTOM LEFT
Williams Island
Dade County, FL

BOTTOM RIGHT
Admiral's Cove
Jupiter, FL
Photo: Arthur J. Pearl

SWEDROE KORN INTERIORS

825 S. Bayshore Drive
Penthouse Tower III
Miami, FL 33131
305 375 8080

FIRM SPECIALTY:
Interior Design

THIS PAGE
The Gables Condominium
Coral Gables, FL 33131

4848 SW 74th Court
Miami, FL 33155
305 663 9688

This Page
Gables Square
Office Building
Coral Gables, FL
Photo: Raul Pedroso

THOMPSON, VENTULETT, STAINBACK & ASSOCIATES

CNN Center,
Twelfth Floor North
Atlanta, GA 30303
404 688 8531

FAR LEFT, TOP
Concourse at
Landmark Center
Atlanta, GA
Photo: E. Alan McGee

FAR LEFT, BOTTOM
Pennsylvania Convention
Center, 1991
Philadelphia, PA
Artist: Joseph N. Smith

FAR LEFT
Oglethorpe Mall, 1990
Savannah, GA
Photo: Gabriel Benzur

TOP
AT&T Inforum, 1990
Atlanta, GA
Photo: Kevin Rose

BOTTOM LEFT
Miami Beach Convention
Center, 1989
Miami Beach, FL
Joint venture with
Borrelli Frankel Blitstein
Architects
Photo: Dan Forer

BOTTOM RIGHT
The World of Coca-Cola
Pavilion, 1990
Atlanta, GA
Photo: Michael Pugh

9-26 Estate Nazareth
St. Thomas, U.S. Virgin
Islands 00802
809 775 7843

FIRM SPECIALTY:
Caribbean Architecture

FAR LEFT
Lundy Residence
St. Thomas,
U.S. Virgin Islands
Photo: Ray Miles

TOP
Sampson Residence
St. Thomas,
U.S. Virgin Islands
Photo: Ray Miles

BOTTOM LEFT
White Residence
St. Thomas,
U.S. Virgin Islands
Photo: D. White

BOTTOM RIGHT
Spinnaker Reef Resort
British Virgin Islands
Photo: Ray Miles

GEORGE F. WHITE AIA & ASSOCIATES, INC.

5455 N. Federal Highway

Boca Raton, FL 33487

407 997 6698

TOP

Interbanc

Ft. Lauderdale, FL

Photo: Michael Decoulos

CENTER

Parker, Johnson, Owen,

McGuire, Michaud, Lang &

Kruppenbacher

Boca Raton, FL

Photo: William H. Sanders

BOTTOM LEFT

Templeton Investment

Counsel, Inc.

Ft. Lauderdale, FL

Photo: Nancy Robinson

Watson

BOTTOM RIGHT

Wellesley Corporate Plaza

Plantation, FL

Photo: William H. Sanders

Index

ALABAMA

S. DAVID BOOZER, Anniston	205 831 8179
35 JULIAN JENKINS, COLOURS, INC., Anniston	**205 237 1607**
LANCASTER & LANCASTER, Auburn	205 887 3406
KEITH McPHEETERS, Auburn	205 887 8779
ADAMS DESIGN ASSOCIATES, Birmingham	205 328 1100
W. SCOTT ANDERTON, Birmingham	205 942 0079
ARCHITECTS SOUTH, Birmingham	205 322 6392
P. LAUREN BARRETT, Birmingham	205 324 7277
RICHARD BARROW, Birmingham	205 254 8037
ROBERT P. BYRAM, Birmingham	205 871 3615
ALBERTO CHIESA, Birmingham	205 252 5901
CRAWFORD McWILLIAMS HATCHER, Birmingham	205 251 3216
DAVIS BLACK & ASSOCIATES, Birmingham	205 871 4285
DAVIS SPEAKE & ASSOCIATES, Birmingham	205 322 7482
GIATTINA FISHER & CO., Birmingham	205 933 9060
GARIKES WILSON ATKINSON, Birmingham	205 252 9191
GREER HOLMQUIST & CHAMBERS, Birmingham	205 251 7241
GRESHAM SMITH & PARTNERS, Birmingham	205 870 4455
HOLLEY & WATSON, Birmingham	205 870 7564
KIDD PLOSSER SPRAGUE, Birmingham	205 251 0125
HENRY SPROTT LONG & ASSOCIATES, Birmingham	205 323 4564
CHARLES H. McCAULEY, Birmingham	205 933 7100
MIMS & GAUNT, Birmingham	205 324 4489
MOODY & ASSOCIATES, Birmingham	205 933 7170
OWENS & WOODS, Birmingham	205 251 8426
OSCAR W. PARDUE, Birmingham	205 979 2663
RENNEKER, TICHANSKY & ASSOCIATES, Birmingham	205 252 5220
ALBIE R. SMITH, Birmingham	205 870 4131
EVAN M. TERRY, Birmingham	205 871 9765
TRO/THE RITCHIE ORGANIZATION, Birmingham	205 324 6744
WATERS/BARROW & ASSOCIATES, Birmingham	205 254 8037
UNDERWOOD ASSOCIATES, Decatur	205 355 1301
BARNES & RITCHIE, Dothan	205 794 7558
HOLMES & GREEN, Dothan	205 794 4178
MILNER, MOORE, MAYNE, Dothan	205 793 7386
LAMBERT EZELL, Florence	205 767 7100
FITZGERALD HILL, Florence	205 766 3824
SMITH, KRANERT, TOMBLIN, Florence	205 764 8861
ROBERT W. WHITTEN, Florence	205 767 6338
RONALD G. CANNON, Gadsden	205 543 3806
FLYNN E. HUDSON, Greensboro	205 624 3426

CROW OVERBEEK NEVILLE PETERS, Huntsville	205 536 0756
FUQUA, HUGHES & OSBORN, Huntsville	205 534 3516
GOODRUM & KNOWLES, Huntsville	205 533 1484
INTERGRAPH, Huntsville	205 730 1958
JONES & HERRIN, Huntsville	205 539 0764
KAMBACK & SIMPSON, Huntsville	205 536 4148
JOE E. MILBERGER & ASSOCIATES, Huntsville	205 534 0657
TOWNSLEY & ASSOCIATES, Huntsville	205 536 9887
DAVID SMITHERMAN, Madison	205 837 3428
THE ARCHITECTS GROUP, Mobile	205 343 1811
ARCHITECTURAL RESOURCES, Mobile	205 690 3496
EDWARD BAUMHAUER, Mobile	205 344 1765
DONNELL & FROOM, Mobile	205 432 8868
HARVEY M. GANDLER, Mobile	205 342 1437
HALL & DENDY, Mobile	205 432 1457
N.H. HOLINES, Mobile	205 432 8871
BARGAINER/McKEE/SIMS, Montgomery	205 834 2038
BORDEN & McKEAN, Montgomery	205 272 4044
BROWN STANSELL, Montgomery	205 277 9020
C. ROBERT CHERRY, Montgomery	205 271 3015
COLE AND HILL, Montgomery	205 270 0227
EDMONDSON & ASSOCIATES, Montgomery	205 262 3868
ROBERT E. JOHNSON ASSOCIATES, Montgomery	205 272 0346
NICHOLS & ASSOCIATES, Montgomery	205 834 9666
J.R. ORTEGA, Montgomery	205 269 2756
PEARSON HUMPHRIES JONES, Montgomery	205 265 8781
RICHARDSON & ASSOCIATES, Montgomery	205 262 3444
SEAY & SEAY, Montgomery	205 263 5162
SHERLOCK, SMITH & ADAMS, Montgomery	205 263 6481
TILLER, BUTNER, ROSA, Montgomery	205 834 6170
WATSON WATSON RUTLAND, Montgomery	205 263 6401
WOODHAM & SHARPE, Montgomery	205 263 7539
LEWIS JONES, Phenix City	205 298 7169
DONALDSON/ARCHITECTS, Sheffield	205 381 5720
ALMON ASSOCIATES, Tuscaloosa	205 349 2100
MAJOR L. HOLLAND, Tuskegee	205 727 4079

ARKANSAS

RANDALL WOLVERTON, Alexander	501 847 8881
HERMAN LEE ARCHITECTS, Batesville	501 793 5711
BARNEY L. ALEXANDER, Benton	501 375 5908
BLACK, CORLEY & ASSOCIATES, Benton	501 778 7686

JOHN C. AYRES, Cabot	501 843 2016	A FINE LINE, Little Rock	501 664 8435
ROBERT M. SCHELLE, ARCHITECT, Cabot	501 843 7931	THE FLETCHER FIRM, Little Rock	501 374 6050
STEVE JORDAN, Camden	501 836 8945	THOMAS JOHNSON ARCHITECT, Little Rock	501 375 0334
THE ROGERS ARCHITECTURAL FIRM, Camden	501 836 8585	LEWIS, ODOM, ELLIOTT & STUDER, Little Rock	501 223 9302
JOHN SANDERS, Camden	501 836 2200	LEWIS ARCHITECTS, Little Rock	501 374 0442
GEORGE ANDERSEN & ASSOCIATES, Conway	501 327 7777	ALLAN L. LILLEY, Little Rock	501 224 9106
ANDREW CLYDE, El Dorado	501 863 8891	MEHLBURGER TANNER ROBINSON, Little Rock	501 375 5331
CONNELLY, ABBOTT & TRULL, El Dorado	501 863 7367	MORRIS FARRAR ARCHITECTS, Little Rock	501 374 3001
GLENN E. LUNDBLAD, Fairfield Bay	501 884 3796	ROARK PERKINS PERRY, Little Rock	501 372 0272
DESIGN DIRECTION, Fayetteville	501 521 9816	POLK STANLEY ASSOCIATES, Little Rock	501 378 0878
HAILEY ASSOCIATES, Fayetteville	501 442 5565	ALLISON MOSES REDDEN, Little Rock	501 375 0378
FAY JONES & MAURICE JENNINGS, Fayetteville	501 443 4742	NATHANIEL, CURTIS, RIDDICK, Little Rock	501 372 2822
JAMES LAMBETH, Fayetteville	501 521 1304	ROUSSEAU, FENNEL & ASSOCIATES, Little Rock	501 372 6734
THE ROGERS COMPANY, Fayetteville	501 521 4756	DAN F. STOWERS, Little Rock	501 376 3277
SMITH & RUSSELL ARCHITECTS, Fayetteville	501 442 9393	THE STUCK ASSOCIATES, Little Rock	501 378 0059
JOHN C. WOMACK, Fayetteville	501 521 5067	WELLBORN, HENDERSON ASSOCIATES, Little Rock	501 374 8254
ANDERSON HUNTER ARCHITECTS, Fort Smith	501 783 0219	WILLIAM WIEDOWER ARCHITECTS, Little Rock	501 375 8252
ARCHITECTURE PLUS, Fort Smith	501 783 8395	THE WILCOX GROUP, Little Rock	501 666 4546
AL DRAP, ARCHITECT, Fort Smith	501 783 3319	WILKINS/SIMS, Little Rock	501 375 3356
DRIMMELL McDANIEL STATON, Fort Smith	501 783 0263	F. EUGENE WITHROW, Little Rock	501 664 6408
THE HILL GROUP, Fort Smith	501 783 0219	WITSELL, EVANS & RASCO, Little Rock	501 374 5300
LANE & ASSOCIATES, Fort Smith	501 782 4277	WITTENBERG, DELONY & DAVIDSON, Little Rock	501 376 6681
LASER/KNIGHT/HENDRIX, Fort Smith	501 782 4085	YOUNG ASSOCIATES, Little Rock	501 565 2056
MOTT MOBLEY McGOWAN & GRIFFIN, Fort Smith	501 782 1051	DAVID WAYNE KINNAIRD, Magnolia	501 234 7773
T.A. RISLEY & ASSOCIATES, Fort Smith	501 452 2636	TERRY COOPER & ASSOCIATES, Mountain Home	501 425 6075
SAXTON SMITH ASSOCIATES, Fort Smith	501 782 5049	RAYMOND BRANTON & ASSOCIATES, North Little Rock	501 753 8193
FRANK McGARY, Heber Springs	501 362 2868	ANDREW HIEGEL, North Little Rock	501 753 4435
HALL & ASSOCIATES, Hot Springs	501 623 3166	MAYES, SUDDERTH & ETHEREDGE, North Little Rock	501 372 0501
TAYLOR KEMPKES ARCHITECTS, Hot Springs	501 624 5679	BURT TAGGART & ASSOCIATES, North Little Rock	501 758 7443
ARNOLD & STACKS, Jonesboro	501 932 5530	AW NELSON, Pine Bluff	501 534 8922
BRACKETT KRENNERICH & ASSOCIATES, Jonesboro	501 932 0571	GEORGE TSCHIEMER, Pine Bluff	501 534 8265
LITTLE MADDOX ARCHITECTS, Jonesboro	501 935 3813	REED WILLIS & ASSOCIATES, Pine Bluff	501 534 2425
THE STUCK ASSOCIATES, Jonesboro	501 932 4271	BENCHMARK GROUP, Rogers	501 636 5004
WILLIAM ASTI, Little Rock	501 663 5003	PERRY BUTCHER & ASSOCIATES, Rogers	501 636 3545
BLASS, CHILCOTE, CARTER, GASKIN, Little Rock	501 376 6671	CRAFTON TULL & ASSOCIATES, Rogers	501 636 4838
BOZEMAN WOOLDRIDGE, Little Rock	501 227 9490	HIGHT & JACKSON ASSOCIATES, Rogers	501 636 4403
BROOKS & JACKSON, Little Rock	501 664 8700	HERB CRUMPTON & ASSOCIATES, Texarkana	501 774 2724
CORNERSTONE ARCHITECTS, Little Rock	501 225 6397	PAT MAGRUDER, West Memphis	501 735 2757
COURTNEY & CONNELL ARCH., Little Rock	501 376 9444		
THE CROMWELL FIRM, Little Rock	501 372 2900	**C A L I F O R N I A**	
DESIGN & CONSTRUCTION, Little Rock	501 663 3208	24/25 ARTHUR ERICKSON ARCHITECTS, Los Angeles	213 278 1915
GORDON DUCKWORTH, Little Rock	501 375 8949	52/53 PERIDIAN, Irvine	714 261 5120

F L O R I D A

MARK HAMPTON, Coconut Grove	305 443 6946
PANCOAST ALBAISA, Coconut Grove	305 442 1193
ROLANDO SILVA, Coconut Grove	305 444 8262
MAX WOLFE STURMAN, Coconut Grove	305 441 1171
KENNETH TREISTER, Coconut Grove	305 858 2416
ARMANDO A. VALDES, Coconut Grove	305 448 2484
DUANY & PLATER ZYBERK, Coconut Grove	305 445 7602
ABBOTT GROUP, Coral Gables	305 445 9421
ARQUITECTONICA, Coral Gables	305 442 9381
LAWRENCE ARRINGTON, Coral Gables	305 255 2140
ANTHONY BELLUSCHI ARCHITECTS, Coral Gables	305 444 7100
BERMELLO, KURKI & VERA, Coral Gables	305 447 0009
10/11 ▶ **GLENN BUFF & PARTNERS, INC., Coral Gables**	**305 667 3109**
IGNACIO CARRERA JUSTIZ, Coral Gables	305 666 7712
DAVID B. CASE, Coral Gables	305 443 7758
CHISHOLM, SANTOS, RAIMUNDEZ, Coral Gables	305 443 9493
FREEDMAN/COHEN, Coral Gables	305 447 9167
H. CARLTON DECKER, Coral Gables	305 444 8288
DE LA LLAMA & ASSOCIATES, Coral Gables	305 665 8233
CARLOS DOMINGUEZ, Coral Gables	305 442 9631
CARLOS M. ESTEVEZ, Coral Gables	305 446 4474
FERGUSON, GLASGOW, SCHUSTER, Coral Gables	305 443 7758
26 ▶ **FILER & HAMMOND ARCHITECTS, INC., Coral Gables**	**305 444 5714**
FULLERTON DIAZ & PARTNERS, Coral Gables	305 442 4200
30/31 ▶ **HARPER CARREÑO MATEU, INC., Coral Gables**	**305 441 0888**
R.J. HEISENBOTTLE, Coral Gables	305 446 7799
MASPONS/GOICOURIA/ESTEVEZ, Coral Gables	305 444 0413
MATTHEWS & ASSOCIATES, Coral Gables	305 446 6199
MUDULOR ARCHITECTS, Coral Gables	305 442 9490
45 ▶ **THE NICHOLS PARTNERSHIP, Coral Gables**	**305 443 5206**
48/49 ▶ **CHARLES HARRISON PAWLEY, Coral Gables**	**305 446 1700**
THEODORE ROUX, Coral Gables	305 443 8115
62/63 ▶ **SASAKI ASSOCIATES, INC., Coral Gables**	**305 661 1346**
WILLIAM TSCHUMY, Coral Gables	305 446 1789
JAMES VENSEL, Coral Gables	305 666 9706
WALLACE ROBERTS & TODD, Coral Gables	305 448 0788
RALPH WARBURTON, Coral Gables	305 667 5185
MAURICE WEINTRAUB, Coral Gables	305 666 8414
KLEMENTS & ASSOCIATES, Coral Gables	305 448 5108
J.S. SCHULTZ, Coral Springs	305 752 0306
DONALD MacNEIR, Dania	305 523 1085
SAM ENGEL, Davie	305 791 4810

ENVIRONMENTAL PLANNING, Davie	305 434 3551
BLAIS & SAYERS, Daytona Beach	904 255 6163
LEETE & LEETE, Daytona Beach	904 253 1785
LARRY ROBINSON, Daytona Beach	904 252 0429
RUSSELL & AXON, Daytona Beach	904 255 5471
FRANCIS WALTON, Daytona Beach	904 258 8615
EDLUND & DRITENBAS, Deerfield Beach	305 429 0995
LEE & SAKAHARA, Deerfield Beach	305 429 1004
LEONARD & BAUGH, Deland	904 734 7977
MacMAHON/CAJACOB, Deland	904 736 2810
NICHOLAS BARBRIE, Delray Beach	407 966 9587
17 ▶ **CURRIE SCHNEIDER ASSOCIATES, Delray Beach**	**407 276 4951**
JAMES JOHNSON, Delray Beach	407 243 1715
ROY M. SIMON, Delray Beach	407 278 1914
DESTIN ARCHITECTURAL GROUP, Destin	904 837 8152
SCHULTZ AND COLLMAN, Dunedin	813 733 0491
7 ▶ **ADACHE ASSOCIATES, Fort Lauderdale**	**305 525 8133**
ATELIER ARCHITECTURE, Fort Lauderdale	305 462 7090
BIGONEY ASSOCIATES, Fort Lauderdale	305 763 5033
GEORGE BUSBY, Fort Lauderdale	305 764 2600
GUSTAVO JOSE CARBONELL, Fort Lauderdale	305 462 6565
RUSSELL C. CHASE, Fort Lauderdale	305 467 7892
CYP OF FLORIDA INC., Fort Lauderdale	305 462 4964
WILLIAM DORSKY ASSOCIATES, Fort Lauderdale	305 373 5384
22/23 ▶ **DAN C. DUCKHAM, Fort Lauderdale**	**305 564 5730**
JEFF FALKANGER & ASSOCIATES, Fort Lauderdale	305 764 6575
GAMBLE, GILROY, MARTIN, MOUL, Fort Lauderdale	305 763 1919
GOLDENHOLZ, FISCHER ARCH., Fort Lauderdale	305 491 8282
LEO HANSEN, Fort Lauderdale	305 527 5973
RANDALL F. KELLER, Fort Lauderdale	305 566 8883
PHILLIP MARTIN, Fort Lauderdale	305 779 7803
WILLIAM LEANDER OSBORN, Fort Lauderdale	305 763 7429
OWEN, POWELL, VANHARREN, Fort Lauderdale	305 566 3251
JOHN K. PAYNE, Fort Lauderdale	305 525 2666
60/61 ▶ **RTKL ASSOCIATES INC., Fort Lauderdale**	**305 764 0500**
RICHARD C. REILLY, Fort Lauderdale	305 565 0341
JAMES RYAN, Fort Lauderdale	305 467 8457
E.H. SAAR, Fort Lauderdale	305 771 1212
MARK L. SALTZ, Fort Lauderdale	305 989 3186
SCHARF AND ASSOCIATES, Fort Lauderdale	305 566 2700
MICHAEL SHIFF & ASSOCIATES, Fort Lauderdale	305 486 7500
DONALD SINGER, Fort Lauderdale	305 463 5672

SZERDI AND ASSOCIATES, Fort Lauderdale	305 467 6699	JEFFREY GROSS, Hollywood	305 925 3964
TUTHILL VICK, Fort Lauderdale	305 527 0007	JAMES M. HARTLEY ARCHITECTS, Hollywood	305 987 3500
OSCAR VAGI AND ASSOCIATES, Fort Lauderdale	305 491 1706	MICHAEL ALLEN MOSHER, Hollywood	305 949 0024
VAUGHN & WUNSCH, Fort Lauderdale	305 462 4111	PHILIP PEARLMAN, Hollywood	305 947 2667
WOLFF/DeCAMILLO, Fort Lauderdale	305 771 2820	SG2 ARCHITECTS, Hollywood	305 921 8112
DONALD F. ZIMMER, Fort Lauderdale	305 493 5082	MERVIN WEINSTEIN, Hollywood	305 987 4598
LEROY K. ALBERT, Fort Myers	813 334 1828	CATALYST REIFF, Hollywood	305 920 4004
ARCHITECTURAL RESOURCES, Fort Myers	813 275 0220	ROBERT BARNES & ASSOCIATES, Homestead	305 247 6150
ALVAH BREITWEISER, Fort Myers	813 482 3500	RON DORRIS ARCHITECTS, Homestead	305 247 8405
BURT, HILL, KOSAR, RITTLEMANN, Fort Myers	813 482 4761	KALINSKI ARCH., Inverness	904 726 4301
RICHARD FABBRO, Fort Myers	813 332 3449	AKEL LOGAN & SHAFER, Jacksonville	904 356 2654
W.R. FRIZZELL ARCHITECTS, Fort Myers	813 939 1220	ALFORD ASSOCIATES, Jacksonville	904 384 8576
GORA/McGAHEY ASSOCIATES, Fort Myers	813 275 0225	BOYER/BOYER/FREEDMAN, Jacksonville	904 398 3922
WILLIAMSON GUILD INC., Fort Myers	813 275 8444	ROBERT C. BROWARD, Jacksonville	904 396 4511
EDWARD HILLSTROM, Fort Myers	813 481 1456	MICHAEL THOMAS BRUCE, Jacksonville	904 737 5701
WILLIAM K. KITCHENS, Fort Myers	813 337 4224	CLEMENTS, RUMPEL, GOODWIN, D'AVI, Jacksonville	904 396 2559
MEB ARCHITECTS, Fort Myers	813 337 0776	MICHAEL DUNLAP, Jacksonville	904 388 9999
PARKER MUDGETT SMITH, Fort Myers	813 332 1171	FISHER & SIMMONS, Jacksonville	904 281 1100
RIVERS & PIGOTT, Fort Myers	813 334 1827	FLEET & ASSOCIATES, Jacksonville	904 262 4473
SCHILLING ASSOCIATES, Fort Myers	813 332 4774	FWA GROUP, Jacksonville	904 353 0050
TITSCH & ASSOCIATES, Fort Myers	813 936 4875	CARL D. GARLINGTON, Jacksonville	904 389 4035
VELLAKE & SPENCER, Fort Myers	813 939 4999	THE HASKELL CO., Jacksonville	904 791 4500
EDGAR A. WILSON ARCHITECTS, Fort Myers	813 334 7141	HUNTER/RS & H, Jacksonville	904 739 2000
ROBERT E. TERRY, Fort Pierce	813 461 3311	MORELLE C. JONES, Jacksonville	904 724 1788
KSD ARCHITECTURAL ASSOCIATES, Fort Walton Beach	904 243 9158	JUNCK & WALKER ARCH., Jacksonville	904 731 4033
QUATRE INC., Fort Walton Beach	904 244 9196	KBJ ARCHITECTS, INC., Jacksonville	904 356 9491
BOYKIN HAYTER ASSOCIATES, Gainesville	904 374 4992	KEMP ASSOCIATES, Jacksonville	904 398 5902
TAMMY L. BULLARD ASSOCIATES, Gainesville	904 373 0861	LANE LEUTHOLD, Jacksonville	904 398 2902
BILL EPPES ARCHITECT, Gainesville	904 375 6191	LAZAR ARCHITECTS, INC., Jacksonville	904 723 3895
FLAD & ASSOCIATES, Gainesville	904 377 6884	ARCHITECT PATRICK McDONALD, Jacksonville	904 268 8188
CHARLES F. HARRINGTON, Gainesville	904 372 4459	McDONALD & GUSTAFSON, Jacksonville	904 743 7792
WK HUNTER, Gainesville	904 373 2501	**42/43** **WILLIAM MORGAN ARCHITECTS, Jacksonville**	**904 356 4195**
MOORE MAY GRAHAM BRAME POOLE, Gainesville	904 372 0425	PAPPAS ASSOCIATES, Jacksonville	904 353 5581
PETER PRUGH, Gainesville	904 375 6191	DRAKE PATTILLO, Jacksonville	904 724 1788
RALPH REEGER, Gainesville	904 371 3068	RICHARD W. PEARSON, Jacksonville	904 398 6397
F. BLAIR REEVES ASSOCIATES, Gainesville	904 376 7303	PEREZ ASSOCIATES, Jacksonville	904 737 4504
CRAIG SALLEY & ASSOCIATES, Gainesville	904 372 8424	POWERS & MERRITT, Jacksonville	904 731 8218
KARL THORNE, Gainesville	904 377 8343	REYNOLDS, SMITH & HILLS, Jacksonville	904 739 2000
HARVEY GROSSMAN, Hialeah	305 685 7465	MADIE RIDER, Jacksonville	904 387 6943
ALBERTO R. LAUDERMAN, Hialeah	305 822 7369	RINK REYNOLDS, Jacksonville	904 396 6353
AA FRIMET, Hollywood	305 920 0021	BERNARD D. SANTOS, Jacksonville	904 725 7861
JEROME GOEBEL, Hollywood	305 920 2120	SAXELBYE, POWELL, ROBERTS, PONDER, Jacksonville	904 354 7728

SHEPARD ASSOCIATES, Jacksonville	904 721 2111	SCHENKEL & SHULTZ, Maitland	407 872 3322
KENNETH SMITH ARCHITECTS, Jacksonville	904 724 4800	SCOTT COMPANIES, Maitland	407 660 2766
J. DOUGLAS SNEAD, Jacksonville	904 724 8740	FRANK SHEEHY, Maitland	407 644 5643
THORSEN & WALLACE, Jacksonville	904 737 7476	HERBERT ROSSER SAVAGE, Marco Island	813 394 1580
CORNEIL E. TORBERT, Jacksonville	904 353 4589	BRIEL, RHAME, POYNTER, HAUSER, Melbourne	407 254 7666
VEENSTRA RINAMAN, Jacksonville	904 723 3895	FUGLEBERG, KOCH, Melbourne	407 768 7887
ROBERT C. WISE, Jacksonville	904 388 1114	THE HARRIS CORPORATION, Melbourne	407 724 3613
THOMAS WOODRUFF, Jacksonville	904 379 2133	VISLAY/CANTELOU & HERRERA, Melbourne	407 259 1525
EMILIO ZELLER, Jacksonville	904 355 6481	ABELE ASSOCIATES, Miami	305 665 6102
CHARLES KING, Jacksonville Beach	904 246 2518	HENRY C. ALEXANDER, Miami	305 552 5200
JOHN M. FOSTER, Jensen Beach	407 334 3388	MANUEL ANGLES, Miami	305 445 3041
M. EUGENE MURPHY, Jensen Beach	407 334 2502	ARCHITECTS INTERNATIONAL, Miami	305 573 2052
KEMP CALER, Jupiter	407 747 7571	ARCHITECTURAL PARTNERSHIP, Miami	305 448 5040
DESIGN PLAN RESEARCH, Jupiter	407 744 7695	ARCHITECTURE MONTENAY, Miami	305 591 7677
GBS, Jupiter	407 747 6330	ARCHITEKNICS, Miami	305 661 5392
WESSEL/TOSCH & ERICKSON, Jupiter	407 747 4950	SCOTT B. ARNOLD, Miami	305 667 7596
EDC, Key Biscayne	305 361 5997	ATLAS & ASSOCIATES, Miami	305 325 0076
ROBERTO J. PESANT, Key Biscayne	305 361 7171	**8 ▶ AXIOMA 3, Miami**	**305 670 0477**
SIGMUND BLUM, Key West	305 294 5539	BALDWIN, SACKMAN, CARRINGTON, Miami	305 666 1144
JOSE GONZALEZ, Key West	305 294 3748	**9 ▶ GIORGIO BALLI, Miami**	**305 661 5839**
CHARLES E. McCOY, Key West	305 296 5123	LES BEILINSON, Miami	305 559 1250
EDWARD PILKINGTON, Lake Wales	813 676 5785	E.C. BEROUNSKY, Miami	305 661 5392
CAPE INTERNATIONAL, Lake Worth	407 967 8739	BORELLI & ASSOCIATES, Miami	305 665 8852
KENDRICK REGNVALL & ASSOCIATES, Lakeland	813 687 3573	BOUTERSE, PEREZ, FABREGAS, Miami	305 348 2211
RENFROE & WHITE, Lakeland	813 683 6768	PAUL BUZINEC, Miami	305 667 9663
W. WADE SETLIFF, Lakeland	813 683 7501	CANO, SOTOLONGO, Miami	305 593 9798
SHERWOOD & SANFORD, Lakeland	813 644 3895	FELIX M. CEPERO ASSOCIATES, Miami	305 441 1551
WARREN H. SMITH, Lakeland	813 644 7568	CHANNING & CHANNING, Miami	305 757 2578
LUDWIG SPIESSL, Lakeland	813 646 1110	SALVADOR CRUXENT, Miami	305 374 0230
STRAUGHN FURR ASSOCIATES, Lakeland	813 665 6205	JAVIER CRUZ, Miami	305 552 1125
SWILLEY, CURTIS, BERTOSSI, Lakeland	813 688 8882	JAMES DEEN, Miami	305 661 5121
ARCHITECTURAL CONCEPTS, Largo	813 584 7178	DeKONSCHIN & ASSOCIATES, Miami	305 270 1289
DONALD R. BUSH ASSOCIATES, Largo	813 586 2105	GERALD F. DeMARCO, Miami	305 661 0286
VICTOR CHODORA, Largo	813 462 6550	FONTANILLS & ASSOCIATES, Miami	305 266 6633
RONALD HOWARD ASSOCIATES, Largo	813 585 6805	FRAGA & FEITO, Miami	305 444 6248
R. ALAN LAUGHLIN, Largo	813 581 8470	EDDY FRANCES, Miami	305 854 4070
LOUIS C. GEORGE, Leesburg	904 787 5554	GELABERT & NAVIA, Miami	305 447 8705
HOFFMAN ASSOCIATES, Lighthouse Point	305 481 9005	CHARLES GILLER, Miami	305 531 0333
CHARLAN BROCK ASSOCIATES, Maitland	407 660 8900	GRAY ASSOCIATES, Miami	305 416 8196
HEIMAN, HURLEY, CHARVAT, PEACOCK, Maitland	407 644 2656	GUTIERREZ ARCHITECTS, Miami	305 238 8949
H. MAXWELL PARISH, Maitland	407 647 0771	HATCHER, ZEIGLER, GUNN, Miami	305 661 5375
POOLE ARCHITECTS & PLANNERS, Maitland	407 660 8800	HNTB ARCHITECTS, Miami	305 592 5930

JAN HOCHSTIM, Miami	305 666 0966	
JAS GROUP, Miami	305 261 3257	
JOHNSON ASSOCIATES, Miami	305 377 0621	
DAVID W. JOHNSON, Miami	305 661 8387	
LOUIS KALLINOSSIS, Miami	305 274 2331	
FRASUER KNIGHT, Miami	305 279 3688	
KOGER GROUP, Miami	305 595 8611	
THOMAS M. KRUEMPELSTAEDTER, Miami	305 446 4362	
LAURENCE LANE, Miami	305 386 5527	
ALDO LASTRA, Miami	305 667 9822	
RICHARD LEVINE & ASSOCIATES, Miami	305 576 0254	
JAMES LYNSKEY ARCHITECT, Miami	305 221 2644	
ELMER MARMORSTEIN, Miami	305 446 1525	
SUZANNE MARTINSON, Miami	305 667 3944	
MC HARRY & ASSOCIATES, Miami	305 445 3765	
McLEON ARCHITECTURAL GROUP, Miami	305 940 9437	
J. MIDDLEBROOKS & ASSOCIATES, Miami	305 771 7594	
MODULUS, INC., Miami	305 576 0808	
OFFERLE & LERNER, Miami	305 385 1700	
JOSEPH PASQUALE, Miami	305 624 7207	
JACQUELINE PEPPER, Miami	305 252 0665	
MANUEL PEREZ VICHOT, Miami	305 575 3406	
RICHARD PLUMER DESIGN, Miami	305 573 5533	
POST BUCKLEY SCHUH JERNIGAN, Miami	305 592 7275	
CRAIG JAMES PRANDINI, Miami	305 665 5436	
LEMUEL RAMOS & ASSOCIATES, Miami	305 666 2884	
RO ARCHITECTS, Miami	305 661 5990	
CHARLES E. RICHTER, Miami	305 592 0589	
H.J. ROSS ASSOCIATES, Miami	305 591 7677	
RUSSELL PARTNERSHIP, Miami	305 441 0268	
RICHARD SCIANDRA, Miami	305 446 9262	
J SCOTT ARCHITECTURE, Miami	305 375 9388	
CHARLES SIEGER, Miami	305 274 2702	
64 **SISKIND-CARLSON & PARTNERS, Miami**	**305 547 1333**	
SMITH, KORACH, HAYET, HAYNIE, Miami	305 552 5200	
SPILLIS CANDELA, Miami	305 444 4691	
70/71 **SWANKE HAYDEN CONNELL ASSOCIATES, Miami**	**305 536 8600**	
TANENBAUM ARCHITECTS, Miami	305 274 6000	
75 **TAQUECHEL-EGUILIOR & ASSOCIATES, Miami**	**305 663 9688**	
TILDEN, TACHI, PALES, Miami	305 579 5901	
TRIMM AND ASSOCIATES, Miami	305 666 2898	
URBANCORE, Miami	305 446 1955	

AJ VERDE, Miami	305 443 1466	
DONALD VIZZA, Miami	305 667 5316	
WADE & KREIDT, Miami	305 444 3360	
WATSON, DEUTSCHMAN, KRUSE, LYONS, Miami	305 871 4084	
JOHN ALBERT WELLER, Miami	305 667 1425	
WEST ARCHITECTS, INC., Miami	305 858 3030	
DANIEL WILLIAMS, Miami	305 858 4144	
WOLFBERG, ALVAREZ, Miami	305 666 5474	
YAROS ARCHITECTS, Miami	305 573 5533	
ZYSCOVICH, INC., Miami	305 372 5222	
MARCUS FRANKEL, Miami Beach	305 538 3663	
GAMBACH ARCHITECTS, Miami Beach	305 932 4940	
GILLER, Miami Beach	305 538 6324	
HENRY B. KONOVER, Miami Beach	305 673 0950	
ISAAC SKLAR & ASSOCIATES, Miami Beach	305 672 8896	
72/73 **SWEDROE ARCHITECTS, Miami Beach**	**305 673 6002**	
RKT & B, Miami Lakes	305 557 4900	
GORDON & ASSOCIATES, Mount Dora	904 383 6505	
ANDREA CLARK BROWN, Naples	813 263 3898	
DON CAHILL, Naples	813 597 6266	
BRUCE CUTLER, Naples	813 598 2413	
MARY C. GESHAY ASSOCIATES, Naples	813 261 8702	
HILLS, GILBERTSON, Naples	813 261 8726	
WALTER L. KELLER, Naples	813 262 7159	
MARIO LAMENDOLA, Naples	813 262 4788	
VAN A. MILLER, Naples	813 262 5082	
RICHARD W. MORRIS, Naples	813 261 7318	
MOYER ARCHITECTS, Naples	813 261 8702	
ROBERT A. PAHL, Naples	813 643 3252	
CHARLES VINCENT ROWE, Naples	813 643 1899	
FREDERICK SWETLAND, Naples	813 263 3573	
CHARLES S. PARTIN, New Port Richie	813 842 9581	
WILLIAM J. MILLER, New Smyrna Beach	904 427 6323	
MORTON Z. LEVINE, Nokomis	813 485 2015	
66/67 **BARRY SUGERMAN, North Miami**	**305 893 6055**	
JEROME H. APPEL, North Miami Beach	305 932 7759	
RALPH CHOEFF, North Miami Beach	305 940 7662	
NUJIM NEPOMECHIE, North Miami Beach	305 651 7182	
ARCHITECTURAL DESIGN ASSOCIATES, North Palm Beach	407 626 7381	
GARY, DYTRYCK, RYAN, North Palm Beach	407 844 3700	
OMURA CASEY INC., North Palm Beach	407 626 1133	
NORMAN ROBSON, North Palm Beach	407 844 4141	

THOMAS BOMBASSEI, Ocala	904 732 4593	
TERRENCE MICHAEL JOHNSON, Ocala	904 351 1963	
BERRY JC WALKER, Ocala	904 622 6237	
BHIDE & HALL ARCHITECTS, Orange Park	904 264 1919	
B. THEODORE COLEMAN, Orange Park	904 264 7801	
A/R/C, Orlando	407 896 7875	
DAVIS & ASSOCIATES, Orlando	407 896 0037	
DONOVAN DEAN & ASSOCIATES, Orlando	407 425 3209	
THE EVANS GROUP, Orlando	407 849 6310	
ALVAH HARDY II, Orlando	407 465 1778	
HANSEN, LIND, MEYER, Orlando	407 422 7061	
C.T. HSU, Orlando	407 423 0098	
HUNTON, BRADY, PRIOR, MASO, Orlando	407 839 0886	
INTERPLAN PRACTICE, Orlando	407 645 5008	
RAY JOHNSON & ASSOCIATES, Orlando	407 843 6614	
MORRIS ARCHITECTS, Orlando	407 839 0414	

52/53 PERIDIAN, Orlando — **407 857 5964**

TRAIAN J. POP, Orlando	407 628 1544	
GEORGE L. POWELL, Orlando	407 142 5461	
ROE/ELISEO, Orlando	407 859 1756	
SCHEMMER ASSOCIATES, Orlando	407 896 0961	
SCHWEITZER INC., Orlando	407 425 0922	

68/69 SVERDRUP CORPORATION, Orlando — **407 875 0222**

EDWARD L. THOMAS, Orlando	407 425 4820	
VOA ASSOCIATES, Orlando	407 425 2500	
WALTON ARCHITECTURAL ASSOCIATES, Orlando	407 423 0627	
WILLIAMS, TREBILCOCK, WHITEHEAD, Orlando	407 423 7862	
GERKEN AND SMITH, Ormond Beach	904 673 1810	
JAMES A. GREENE, Oviedo	407 365 1192	
DOUGLAS HODGE, Palatka	904 328 3553	
ROBERT E. TAYLOR, Palatka	904 325 7341	
JOHN F. COLAMARINO, Palm Beach	407 832 0009	
STEEL ASSOCIATES, Palm Beach	407 833 7445	
LEMBO & ASSOCIATES, Palm Harbor	813 785 7922	
PILOT CORPORATION, Palm Harbor	813 785 5433	
ALEXANDER RAYMOND, Palm Harbor	813 786 1937	
UGARTE & ASSOCIATES, Palmetto	813 729 5691	
COLLINS & ASSOCIATES, Panama City	904 769 3357	
SINAN INC., Panama City	904 785 9911	
AMSPACHER & AMSPACHER, Pensacola	904 434 0123	
BULLOCK AND TICE, Pensacola	904 434 5444	
CARDWELL JERNIGAN ASSOCIATES, Pensacola	904 478 8453	

WILLIAM GRAVES, Pensacola	904 432 1912
HTC DAVIS, Pensacola	904 433 7062
HUGH LEITCH, Pensacola	904 432 6196
DONALD R. LINDSEY, Pensacola	904 434 5179
SONSHIP ARCHITECTS, Pensacola	904 478 1053
KENNETH WOOLF, Pensacola	904 438 3653
ETW & ASSOCIATES, Plantation	305 584 1224
RONALD KALL, Plantation	305 587 0404
FRANZ JOSEPH SHROPA, Plantation	305 584 7700
T. AMLIE, Pompano Beach	305 972 3300
AMS ARCHITECTS, Pompano Beach	305 973 3997
DK ARCHITECTS, Pompano Beach	305 941 3055
FPA CORP., Pompano Beach	305 975 6007
BERNARD ROWAN, Punta Gorda	813 637 1244
WALKER AND ASSOCIATES, Safety Harbor	813 799 6480
FENTON ASSOCIATES, Sanibel	813 472 9113
CARL ABBOTT, Sarasota	813 351 5016
BRUCE BALK, Sarasota	813 366 3300
STUART H. BARGER, Sarasota	813 365 6056
BLIVAS FIALA ROWE & ASSOCIATES, Sarasota	813 952 1963
DIVERSIFIED DESIGN, Sarasota	813 749 1263
DREHER ARCHITECTS, Sarasota	813 955 9883
FRANK FOLSOM SMITH & PARTNERS, Sarasota	813 365 7336
RICHARD M. GARFINKEL, Sarasota	813 366 7755
WM. THORNING LITTLE, Sarasota	813 365 9284
PADGETT RITTER HARRIS, Sarasota	813 955 8370
GEORGE PALERMO, Sarasota	813 955 0301
PANDORA SEIBERT, Sarasota	813 366 9161
BRENT PARKER, Sarasota	813 366 2477
THE RITCHIE ORGANIZATION, Sarasota	813 923 4911
SKIRBALL GROUP, Sarasota	813 951 1777
TICHENOR & LINDER, Sarasota	813 366 3777
WEST & CONYERS, Sarasota	813 955 2341
DON WILKINSON, Sarasota	813 953 6069
ZOLLER ASSOCIATES, Sarasota	813 371 4600
STEVEN SCHUYLER, St. Augustine	904 829 3091
FESKO & WILLINGHAM, St. Petersburg	813 821 3445
ANDERSON/PARRISH, St. Petersburg	813 576 1041
ROBERT J. BITTERLI, St. Petersburg	813 527 3412
KATHERINE L. DURHAM, St. Petersburg	813 822 5174
ROBERT B. GREENBAUM, St. Petersburg	813 345 0055
HARVARD, JOLLY, MARCET, St. Petersburg	813 896 4611

JONES ARCHITECTURAL CORP., St. Petersburg	813 393 8063
KIMBROUGH ASSOCIATES, St. Petersburg	813 384 1844
RICHARD LUX, St. Petersburg	813 521 3729
PHILIPPI ASSOCIATES, St. Petersburg	813 397 8948
RENKER EICK PARKS ARCH., St. Petersburg	813 821 2986
F. WILLIAM VOLK, St. Petersburg	813 393 5125
WEDDING & ASSOCIATES, St. Petersburg	813 527 1183
GEORGE YOUNG, St. Petersburg	813 822 4317
WALTER H. MELODY, St. Petersburg	813 393 1354
BRADEN & BRADEN, Stuart	407 287 8258
DAVID DEINARD, Stuart	407 287 6000
RICHARD GRANFIELD, Stuart	407 283 6032
PETER JEFFERSON, Stuart	407 287 5755
DIMITER STOYANOFF, Stuart	407 283 7512
JOHN DIEHL ASSOCIATES, Sunrise	305 973 4747
BARNETT & FRONCZAK, Tallahassee	904 224 6301
BARRETT/DAFFIN/CARLAN, Tallahassee	904 433 5601
CHARLES J. BENDA, Tallahassee	904 878 4163
DONALD BIZZELL, Tallahassee	904 488 9042
BRIEL RHAME POYNTER HOUSER, Tallahassee	904 877 8318
CLEMONS RUTHERFORD, Tallahassee	904 385 6153
CONN ASSOCIATES, Tallahassee	904 385 7454
CROWE AND ASSOCIATES, Tallahassee	904 656 6888
ELLIOTT AND MARSHALL, Tallahassee	904 222 7442
ERVIN AND DAVIS, Tallahassee	904 224 7650
MAYS LEROY GRAY, Tallahassee	904 224 5218
MARK GRIESBACH, Tallahassee	904 222 3970
JOHNSON PETERSON HOLLIDAY, Tallahassee	904 877 3700
MANAUSA AND LEWIS, Tallahassee	904 385 9200
HAROLD ODOM, Tallahassee	904 386 1398
SAXON POYNER, Tallahassee	904 224 5227
JIM ROBERSON & ASSOCIATES, Tallahassee	904 878 7891
A&E DESIGN, Tampa	813 885 4605
THE JAN ABELL GARCIA PARTNERSHIP, Tampa	813 251 3652
CARLOS ALFONSO, Tampa	813 221 3399
ARCHITECTURA, Tampa	813 251 1193
THE ARCHITECTS STUDIO, Tampa	813 223 5200
ASSOCIATED SPACE DESIGN, Tampa	813 223 2293
EUGENE BEACH, Tampa	813 985 4483
BLOODGOOD ARCHITECTS, Tampa	813 286 8414
BRUCE, SHORT, BROOKS ARCHITECTS, Tampa	813 885 8708
BSC DESIGN, Tampa	813 879 3785

CONSOLIDATED ASSOCIATES, Tampa	813 933 8008
COOPER JOHNSON ARCHITECTS, Tampa	813 253 2616
CURRY SMITH JAUDON, Tampa	813 876 1620
DELTA CORPORATION, Tampa	813 621 7900
DESIGN ADVOCATES, Tampa	813 226 2626
DSA GROUP, Tampa	813 870 8670
EDUCATED DESIGN, Tampa	813 289 9000
ELLERBE ARCHITECTS, Tampa	813 229 3538
EXCEL ASSOCIATES, Tampa	813 875 4500
FLEISCHMAN, GARCIA, Tampa	813 251 4400
FLETCHER, VALENTI, CHILLURA, Tampa	813 875 8450
MARK S. HARTLEY, Tampa	813 626 6019
HARVARD, JOLLY, MARCET, ASSOCIATES, Tampa	813 286 8206
32/33 **HELLMUTH, OBATA & KASSABAUM, Tampa**	**813 281 0533**
HENDERSON ASSOCIATES, Tampa	813 251 2441
WILLIAM HENRY, Tampa	813 886 1296
JOHN HOWEY, Tampa	813 223 5396
HUNTER/RSH, Tampa	813 289 5550
INTERARCH DESIGN, Tampa	813 229 8255
JOHNSTON DANA INC., Tampa	813 870 1772
THE MacEWEN GROUP, Tampa	813 253 0421
McELVEY, JENNEWEIN, STEFANY, HOWARD, Tampa	813 223 3516
ODELL ASSOCIATES, Tampa	813 273 9761
MICHAEL PATTERSON, Tampa	813 238 8187
PRIME DESIGN, INC., Tampa	813 289 3313
RANON & PARTNERS, INC., Tampa	813 253 3465
RENALDO CRISWELL ASSOCIATES, Tampa	813 289 8516
H. GLEN RICHMOND, Tampa	813 831 1520
ROBBINS BELL & KEUHLEM, Tampa	813 223 2771
ROWE HOLMES BARNETT, Tampa	813 221 9771
JAMES DOUGLAS RUYLE, Tampa	813 885 6633
PHILIP SCALERA, Tampa	813 932 0700
SMITH BARNES ARCHITECTURE, Tampa	813 251 1884
65 **SMALLWOOD, REYNOLDS, STEWART, STEWART & ASSOC., Tampa**	**813 221 1226**
EUGENE R. SMITH & ASSOCIATES, Tampa	813 961 8757
SPACE DESIGN INTERNATIONAL, Tampa	813 273 0362
THE STEWART CORPORATION, Tampa	813 223 2741
SZUMLIC WITHERS GROUP, Tampa	813 831 8999
STANSELL TENNISON, Tampa	813 228 7652
H. LESLIE WALKER, Tampa	813 886 5931
WOODROFFE CORPORATION, Tampa	813 253 2002
REEFE YAMADA ASSOCIATES, Tampa	813 875 9656

	MANUEL DEL CAMPO, Tarpon Springs	813 943 2611
	EDWARD C. HOFFMAN, Tarpon Springs	813 923 2835
	ROBERT PETTIGREW, Valrico	813 689 9628
	HIBNER & LEVINE ASSOCIATES, Venice	813 484 9333
	CHARLES BLOCK, Vero Beach	407 569 3799
	GEORGE F. BOLLIS, Vero Beach	407 567 8782
	JOHN CALMES, Vero Beach	407 567 1402
	JOHN H. DEAN, Vero Beach	407 567 4907
	EDLUND & DRITENBAS, Vero Beach	407 569 4320
27	**GIBSON & SILKWORTH ARCHITECTS, Vero Beach**	**407 231 6008**
	MATTHEW GORE, Vero Beach	407 567 2002
	DAVID V. ROBISON, Vero Beach	407 567 5224
	CLEMENS BRUNS SCHAUB, Vero Beach	407 231 1484
	ARCHITECTS SCHLITT & BRENNER, Vero Beach	407 562 1716
	ANSTIS & ORNSTEIN, West Palm Beach	407 844 7070
	FREDERICK ASTLE, West Palm Beach	407 689 4962
	STEVEN BRUH, West Palm Beach	407 689 3521
	LESLIE DiVOLL INC., West Palm Beach	407 471 1668
	ALDEN B. DOW, West Palm Beach	407 655 2858
	EDGE GROUP, West Palm Beach	407 585 9307
	FANNING, HOWEY, West Palm Beach	407 697 2800
	GEE & JENSON, West Palm Beach	407 683 3301
	GINOCCHIO AND SPINO, West Palm Beach	407 686 4405
	MARION & PALUGA, West Palm Beach	407 683 7000
	FRAN MURPHY INC., West Palm Beach	407 659 6202
	OLIVER & GLIDDEN, West Palm Beach	407 684 6841
46/47	**THE PANDULA ARCHITECTS, INC., West Palm Beach**	**407 832 3614**
	PEACOCK AND LEWIS, West Palm Beach	407 655 4063
	PECHT & WENSING, West Palm Beach	407 832 5501
	SCHWARD AND TWITTY, West Palm Beach	407 832 5599
	SMITH, OBST, West Palm Beach	407 064 8700
	TREZISE DESIGN ASSOCIATES, West Palm Beach	407 649 6962
	ROBERT L. VICKERS, West Palm Beach	407 471 5333
	GEORGE K. WASSER, West Palm Beach	407 686 7800
	GENE LEEDY, Winter Haven	813 293 7173
	ARCHITECTS DESIGN GROUP, Winter Park	407 647 1706
	DAVIS & ASSOCIATES, Winter Park	407 896 0037
	DUER & BLACKMAN, Winter Park	407 647 0823
	FUGLEBERG KOCH ARCHITECTS, Winter Park	407 629 0595
	ROBERT A. HARRIS, Winter Park	407 647 7340
	HWH ARCHITECTS, Winter Park	407 423 5525
	LOPATKA, MURDOCK, JAMMAL, PARSONS, Winter Park	407 644 6777
	THE NASRALLAH CORPORATION, Winter Park	407 876 1945
	PDR ARCHITECTS, Winter Park,	407 628 0620
	ROGERS, LOVELOCK, FRITZ, Winter Park	407 647 1039
	STUDIO 7, Winter Park	407 647 8778
	RICK SWISHER, Winter Park	407 644 3003
	JOHN H. VON GUNTEN, Winter Park	407 869 5559
	HAMPTON/MONDAY ARCHS., Winter Park	407 644 2606

G E O R G I A

	WILLIAM COX, Albany	912 435 5419
	SAUNDERS ASSOCIATES, Albany	912 436 9877
	YIELDING, WAKEFORD & ZANARDO, Albany	912 435 0036
	WOOD C. CAMPBELL, Athens	404 353 2933
	JOHN W. LINLEY, Athens	404 542 1816
	AECK ASSOCIATES, Atlanta	404 522 5719
	AIGROUP ARCHITECTS, Atlanta	404 873 2555
	AIKEN AIKEN & SHEETZ, Atlanta	404 233 4466
	ALDERMAN AND GRAHAM, Atlanta	404 454 9121
	ALLAIN & ASSOCIATES INC., Atlanta	404 872 2494
	ALSBROOKS ASSOCIATES, Atlanta	404 876 1007
	ANTHONY AMES, Atlanta	404 266 8904
	TAYLOR ANDERSON, ARCHITECTS, Atlanta	404 237 4725
	ARCHITECTURE INTERNATIONAL, Atlanta	404 873 2555
	ARCHITECTS PLUS, Atlanta	404 449 6330
	ARKHORA ASSOCIATES, Atlanta	404 872 2217
	ARNOLD & SPIESS, Atlanta	404 873 1723
	ASSOCIATED SPACE DESIGN, Atlanta	404 688 3318
	BARKER, CUNNINGHAM, BARRINGTON, Atlanta	404 255 6260
	BARRETT AND ASSOCIATES, Atlanta	404 394 4540
	BLOUNT PITTMAN, Atlanta	404 874 1148
	BRADFIELD ASSOCIATES, Atlanta	404 231 5202
	BULL & KENNEY, Atlanta	404 873 3353
	WADE BURNS, Atlanta	404 752 7300
	CAMP ARCHITECTS, Atlanta	404 523 2509
15	**CAMPBELL POPE & ASSOCIATES, INC., Atlanta**	**404 233 6847**
	CARLSTEN ASSOCIATES, Atlanta	404 589 0404
	CHAPMAN, COYLE & CHAPMAN, Atlanta	404 952 2952
	RICHARD CHEATHAM, Atlanta	404 378 6405
	COMBS & GUILD, Atlanta	404 876 3612
	COOPER CARRY & ASSOCIATES INC., Atlanta	404 237 2000
	A. BURNHAM COOPER, Atlanta	404 261 8748
	CUNNINGHAM FOREHAND MATTHEWS & MOORE, Atlanta	404 873 2152

LP DAHR ARCHITECTS, Atlanta	404 434 0105
LEO DALY, Atlanta	404 980 1190
DANIELSON & PAINE & ASSOCIATES, Atlanta	404 252 0120
DEAN DESIGNS, Atlanta	404 262 9173
DECKBAR McCORMACK, INC., Atlanta	404 633 9406
21 DIEDRICH ARCHITECTS & ASSOCIATES, Atlanta	**404 364 9633**
ELLIOTT ASSOCIATES, Atlanta	404 436 8911
WARREN EPSTEIN & ASSOCIATES, Atlanta	404 873 5111
MARSHALL ERDMAN AND ASSOCIATES, Atlanta	404 451 2752
FERNANDEZ ASSOCIATES ARCHITECT, Atlanta	404 457 2500
FISCHER ORGANIZATION LTD., Atlanta	404 231 0110
GARDNER, SPENCER, SMITH & ASSOCIATES, Atlanta	404 446 0944
GEHEBER LEWIS, Atlanta	404 873 3697
GODWIN & ASSOCIATES, Atlanta	404 233 8507
GREENBERG FARROW ARCHITECTS, Atlanta	404 237 5297
KNOX A. GRIFFIN, Atlanta	404 351 8328
HALL, NORRIS & MARSH, INC., Atlanta	404 875 7982
PETER H. HAND ASSOCIATES, Atlanta	404 876 3720
THE HAUSEMAN GROUP, Atlanta	404 231 5900
HEERY INTERNATIONAL INC., Atlanta	404 881 9880
HICKEY, PLATT ASSOCIATES, INC., Atlanta	404 998 3649
DAVID H. HICKS, ARCHITECT, Atlanta	404 378 4829
H. LLOYD HILL ARCHITECT & ASSOCIATES, Atlanta	404 457 4324
BENJAMIN HIRSCH & ASSOCIATES, Atlanta	404 325 3001
HARRY W. HOWELL & ASSOCIATES, Atlanta	404 266 9631
HUGHES/DURFEE, Atlanta	404 894 4873
HUNT/ENLOE/MACKINNON INC., Atlanta	404 320 7100
JOVA DANIELS BUSBY INC., Atlanta	404 892 2890
KELLY LUNDSTROM PRESSLEY, Atlanta	404 881 6565
THE KIRKLAND GROUP, Atlanta	404 892 4000
KOETS CORPORATION, Atlanta	404 231 4554
KRA INC., Atlanta	404 589 8522
GEORGE W. LENTZ, ARCHITECT, Atlanta	404 396 4124
TED LEVY, ARCHITECT, Atlanta	404 892 1244
LORD & SARGENT, Atlanta	404 524 1717
FORREST LOTT, Atlanta	404 234 5230
DENNIS J. MAKUTA, ARCHITECTS, Atlanta	404 897 1615
MASTIN ASSOCIATES, Atlanta	404 237 8268
MAYES, SUDDERTH, Atlanta	404 952 0011
WS McDUFFIE, Atlanta	404 659 5764
JOHN W. McINTOSH, Atlanta	404 262 2813
ROB MILLER, ARCHITECT, Atlanta	404 876 0255

MILLKEY & BROWN, Atlanta	404 522 4310
MOORE/ARCHITECTURE, Atlanta	404 881 1005
MULDAWER MOULTRIE ARCHITECTS, Atlanta	404 239 0914
NICHOLS CARTER GRANT, Atlanta	404 892 4510
NILES BOLTON ASSOCIATES INC., Atlanta	404 365 7600
NIX, MANN & ASSOCIATES, Atlanta	404 872 2800
THE NORRIS GROUP, Atlanta	404 261 0190
OAKDALE ARCHITECTURE, Atlanta	404 892 5825
OSGOOD ADAMS & ASSOCIATES INC., Atlanta	404 688 3600
PALMER FLYNN FINDERUP ARCHITECTS, Atlanta	404 843 0075
PARSONS, BRINCKERHOFF, QUADE, Atlanta	404 237 2115
MILTON PATE & ASSOCIATES, INC., Atlanta	404 633 4586
JAMES PATTERSON ASSOCIATES, Atlanta	404 881 8066
JOSEPH PERRY ASSOCIATES, INC., Atlanta	404 231 1521
GINI L. PETTUS, Atlanta	404 876 6880
PM ARCHITECTS, Atlanta	404 980 0020
54/55 PORTMAN FRUCHTMAN VINSON ARCHITECTS, INC., Atlanta	**404 859 0323**
56/57 JOHN PORTMAN ASSOCIATES, Atlanta	**404 522 8811**
PRESNELL ASSOCIATES, Atlanta	404 455 9375
KAREL PRUNER ASSOCIATES, INC., Atlanta	404 955 6964
PUCCIANO & ENGLISH, INC., Atlanta	404 457 0623
WILLIAM L. PULGRAM, Atlanta	404 255 8514
QUANTRELL MULLINS, Atlanta	404 874 6048
RABUN HATCH & ASSOCIATES, Atlanta	404 876 8125
RICHARD RAUH & ASSOCIATES, Atlanta	404 233 9447
REYNOLDS, SMITH & HILLS, Atlanta	404 320 1308
SY RICHARDS, ARCHITECT, INC., Atlanta	404 633 2677
ROBERT AND CO., Atlanta	404 577 4000
J.W. ROBINSON & ASSOCIATES, INC., Atlanta	404 753 4129
ROSSER FABRAP INTERNATIONAL, Atlanta	404 688 3596
RICHARD ROTHMAN, Atlanta	404 523 8038
RUYS & COMPANY, Atlanta	404 231 3572
GUY H. SCHNEIDER, Atlanta	404 396 7449
SCOGIN ELAM AND BRAY, ARCHITECTS, Atlanta	404 350 0488
L. WARD SEYMOUR/ARCHITECTURE, Atlanta	404 872 4600
L. MILES SHEFFER, P.C., Atlanta	404 875 6622
SHERRY ASSOCIATES, ARCHITECTS, Atlanta	404 255 2069
RICHARD M. SIBLY & ASSOCIATES, INC., Atlanta	404 325 2144
SIZEMORE FLOYD ARCHITECTS, Atlanta	404 233 7888
65 SMALLWOOD, REYNOLDS, STEWART, STEWART & ASSOC. Atlanta	**404 233 5453**
SMITH DALIA ARCHITECTS, Atlanta	404 873 4195
HENRY HOWARD SMITH, ARCHITECT, Atlanta	404 355 8183

FRANK H. SMITH, Atlanta	404 237 7750
STANG & NEWDOW, Atlanta	404 584 0500
STEVENS & WILKINSON, Atlanta	404 688 3990
JAMES E. STRACK & ASSOCIATES, Atlanta	404 876 0101
JOHN H. SUMMER & ASSOCIATES, INC., Atlanta	404 321 0666
SURBER, BARBER, MOONEY, Atlanta	404 874 2400
TAYLOR & WILLIAMS, ARCHITECT, P.C., Atlanta	404 261 2724
TAYLOR ASSOCIATES, P.C., Atlanta	404 261 5772
L. JACK THOMAS, JR., ARCHITECT, Atlanta	404 237 2632
76/77 THOMPSON, VENTULETT, STAINBACK & ASSOC., Atlanta	**404 688 8531**
THOMPSON HANCOCK & WITTE, Atlanta	404 252 8040
TIPPET & ASSOCIATES, Atlanta	404 233 2875
TIPTON MASTERSON ASSOCIATES, Atlanta	404 953 1533
TODD ARCHITECTS, Atlanta	404 458 1448
TOMBERLIN ASSOCIATES, Atlanta	404 451 7531
TOOMBS AMISANO & WELLS INC., Atlanta	404 351 6694
H. PAUL TUGGLE ASSOCIATES, INC., Atlanta	404 633 9406
URBAN CONCEPTS ARCHITECTS, INC., Atlanta	404 491 0713
VANN AND PARTNERS, Atlanta	404 256 0772
WEAVER & WITHERS, INC., Atlanta	404 252 9704
IRV WEINER & ASSOCIATES, Atlanta	404 525 8445
WHATLEY & PARTNERS, Atlanta	404 266 8770
WILLIAMS, RUSSELL, JOHNSON, Atlanta	404 853 6800
EDWARD C. WUNDRAM, ARCHITECT, Atlanta	404 220 0361
WURZ, WISECARVER, PRUETT, INC., Atlanta	404 434 4444
MAURICE YATES, Atlanta	404 255 0385
YEUNG & VINESS, INC., Atlanta	404 261 4343
THE ZENNER GROUP, Atlanta	404 874 5009
SANDEFORD & WEBB, INC., Augusta	404 733 0555
BROWN AND SIGG, Augusta	404 738 5891
NICHOLAS DICKINSON & ASSOCIATES, Augusta	404 722 7488
HOLROYD JOHNSON AND PARTNERS, Augusta	404 724 6180
DORT B. PAYNE, Augusta	404 724 2475
E. L. PERRY, ARCHITECT, Augusta	404 738 4549
WELLS, LAW & HINMAN, Augusta	404 722 3052
THE WOODHURST PARTNERSHIP, Augusta	404 724 4343
BRYANT ARCHITECT, LTD., Avondale Estate	404 296 2533
JG KWILECKI, Bainbridge	912 246 1343
E. JULIAN FLEXER & ASSOCIATES, P.C., Brunswick	404 264 9228
W.S. LEDBETTER, INC., Brunswick	404 265 3907
JOSEPH L. SCHLOSSER, ARCHITECT, Brunswick	404 265 8988
ALEX ROUSH, INC., Carrollton	404 836 1818

BRACKETT ASSOCIATES, Cartersville	404 382 1058
GLENN GRIFFIN ARCHITECTS, Columbus	404 322 1549
HECHT, BURDESHAW AND JOHNSON, Columbus	404 323 1814
WH HOGENCAMP, Columbus	404 323 3806
KERSEY, LUTTRELL & ASSOCIATES, Columbus	404 563 1102
NEAL AND GREENE, Columbus	404 563 4474
KIRKMAN ASSOCIATES, INC., Dalton	404 226 5412
WILLIAM BREEN, Decatur	404 378 0326
RL BROWN, Decatur	404 377 2460
JOSEPH F. DICKS, ARCHITECT, Decatur	404 371 0878
THOMAS E. GARNER, Decatur	404 377 7914
SHEILA A. HUNT, Decatur	404 371 8137
DERYCK MUEHLHAUSER, ARCHITECT, Decatur	404 296 8524
MAYTON ASSOCIATES, Doraville	404 441 0150
H ELTON THOMPSON, Douglasville	404 942 3930
ARTHUR KISER, East Point	404 767 7462
RICHARD LANDAU, Ellijay	404 233 1141
H. LLOYD HILL, ARCHITECT, Gainesville	404 534 8404
JACOBS ARCHITECTS INC., Gainesville	404 535 1133
JAEGER/PYBURN, Gainesville	404 534 7024
REYNOLDS ARCHITECTS, Gainesville	404 531 0100
SPANGLER AND MANLEY ARCHITECTS, Griffin	404 227 5473
ENVIRONMENTAL CONCEPTS, INC., Lawrenceville	404 962 2354
LAWRENCE ENTERPRISES, Lawrenceville	404 963 6723
WINFORD LINDSAY ASSOCIATES, INC., Lawrenceville	404 963 8989
DAVID L. HOLLOWAY & ASSOCIATES, Lilburn	404 979 8122
A. STANFORD ADAMS, ARCHITECT, Macon	912 745 1167
BALIAN & ASSOCIATES, INC., Macon	912 746 1208
BRITTAIN THOMPSON & BRAY, Macon	912 742 1208
JAMES YATES BRUCE, ARCHITECT, Macon	912 742 4678
HENRY CORSINI, ARCHITECT, INC., Macon	912 746 4858
WILLIAM DELOACH, ARCHITECT, Macon	912 742 4999
JOHN DENNIS, JR., ARCHITECT, Macon	912 477 3483
DENNIS & DENNIS, INC., Macon	912 742 2561
DUNWODY, BEELAND & HENDERSON, Macon	912 742 5321
HOLLIDAY, COUCH, HOLLIS & JELK, Macon	912 745 6514
JEAN LEAGUE NEWTON, Macon	912 477 0173
DAVID RICHARDSON ARCHITECT, Macon	912 746 5189
SIDES & POPE, P.C., Macon	912 746 9344
STEPHENS, SMITH & ASSOCIATES, Macon	912 746 7348
WOOD MORRIS & McTIER, INC., Macon	912 745 4945
CARGILL ARCHITECTS, Marietta	404 993 3812

PHILIP CARNES & ASSOCIATES, Marietta	404 953 0223
CHEGWIDDEN DORSEY HOLMES, Marietta	404 423 0016
HALEY & HOWARD, Marietta	404 424 8606
WILLIAM HOWELL AND ASSOCIATES, Marietta	404 955 5365
ARIE KOHN ARCHITECTS P.C., Marietta	404 952 1995
GEORGE MELVIN, Marietta	404 993 3937
WILLIAM R. TAPP, JR., ARCHITECT, Marietta	404 427 5339
TODD ARCHITECTS, INC., Marietta	404 587 5592
E. H. BLACKBURN & ASSOCIATES, Monroe	404 267 8126
WM. FRANK McCALL, JR., Moultrie	912 985 2038
JACK WILSON RANDOLPH, Moultrie	912 985 9868
ARCHITECTS PLUS, Norcross	404 449 6330
CHERRY/ROBERTS/SULLIVAN, Norcross	404 446 3313
JAMES R. LANKFORD, Norcross	404 446 2039
JERRY L. NUZNOV ASSOCIATES, Norcross	404 449 5011
PHILIP B. WINDSOR CO., Norcross	404 447 9834
YIELDING WAKEFORD & ZANARDO, Norcross	404 441 9171
J. DAVID MULLINS, Peachtree City	404 487 4131
ROSS ANDREWS, Ringgold	404 935 6344
DOYLE L. HARVEY, Rome	404 291 8155
BOBBY J. TOLES, Rome	404 234 4816
M.G. TURNER ARCHITECTS & ASSOCIATES, Rome	404 232 4453
BECKETT, PLESS & ASSOCIATES, Roswell	404 992 2664
JACK RICHARDSON FRYE, Roswell	404 992 5662
ZACHARY W. HENDERSON, Roswell	404 992 3308
CLIFFORD A. NAHSER, ARCHITECT, Roswell	404 641 8210
WRIGHT & MITCHELL ASSOCIATES, Roswell	404 998 8059
L. SCOTT BARNARD & ASSOCIATES, Savannah	912 232 6173
GUNN & MEYERHOFF ARCHITECT, Savannah	912 232 1151
HANSEN ARCHITECTS, P.C., Savannah	912 234 8056
RONALD KOLMAN, ARCHITECT, Savannah	912 233 9003
LEVY & KILEY, ARCHITECTS, Savannah	912 232 1603
MADDOX AND ASSOCIATES, P.C., Savannah	912 233 4751
NOWELL & ASSOCIATES, Savannah	912 352 3348
JOHN REITER, Savannah	912 232 4403
BENJAMIN P. RITZERT, ARCHITECT, Savannah	912 355 4382
THOMAS E. STANLEY, Savannah	912 233 6638
JOHN M. MILES, Snellville	404 972 5650
WILLIAM P. HOOKER, St. Simons Island	912 638 2838
USSERY/RULE ARCHITECTS, P.C., St. Simons Island	912 638 6688
LAMAR WEBB ASSOCIATES, St. Simons Island	912 638 8621
DENNIS M. WILLIAMS, ARCHITECT, St. Simons Island	912 638 4555

FRED HAROLD CURLIN, Statesboro	912 764 5550
EDWIN CLIFFORD ECKLES, Statesboro	912 764 6288
JINRIGHT AND RYAN, Thomasville	912 226 1821
BAILEY AND ASSOCIATES, Valdosta	912 247 3535
IPG INCORPORATED, Valdosta	912 242 3557
McCALL GREGORY & ASSOCIATES, Valdosta	912 242 2551
ELLIS RICKET & ASSOCIATES, Valdosta	912 242 3556
SMITH & SMITH, Valdosta	912 244 1174
THOMSON & ASSOCIATES, Valdosta	912 244 0592
STERLING WILHOIT, Watkinsville	404 769 6389
JOHN T. HUFF, ARCHITECT, Waycross	912 285 5807
GARY P. PARKER & ASSOCIATES, Woodstock	404 928 1141

L O U I S I A N A

DOUGLAS ASHE, Alexandria	318 473 0252
BARRON, HEINBERG & BROCATO, Alexandria	318 443 7291
LEWIS R. BROWN, Alexandria	318 445 3151
LYLE BUFKIN, Alexandria	318 445 4108
HAROLD L. DEKEYZER, Alexandria	318 442 6642
JOE FRYAR ARCHITECT, Alexandria	318 445 3328
GLANKER & ASSOCIATES, Alexandria	318 445 3646
ABIDE & ASSOCIATES, Baton Rouge	504 769 5352
AE PLUS, INC., Baton Rouge	504 292 4485
THE AGUILAR GROUP INC., Baton Rouge	504 927 6885
ARCHITECTURAL COLLAB, Baton Rouge	504 345 2300
THE ARCHITECTURE GROUP, Baton Rouge	504 922 4070
C. ROBERT ARNOLD, Baton Rouge	504 344 6580
BANI & CARVILLE ARCHITECTS, Baton Rouge	504 343 2267
EDWARD BENTIN ARCHITECT, Baton Rouge	504 343 4814
BODMAN, WEBB, NOLAND & GUIDROZ, Baton Rouge	504 923 3181
BRADLEY, MIREMONT, BLEWSTER, Baton Rouge	504 346 0650
BRINSON & BETTS ARCHITECTS, Baton Rouge	504 926 5045
THADDEUS A. BROUSSARD ARCHITECT, Baton Rouge	504 343 3407
BROWN & BROWN, Baton Rouge	504 925 8176
FRED L. BUZZELL ARCHITECT, Baton Rouge	504 383 0763
JERRY M. CAMPBELL ARCHITECTS, Baton Rouge	504 381 9435
JOHN J. CAPDEVIELLE ARCHITECT, Baton Rouge	504 768 7719
AMY CARBONETTE, Baton Rouge	504 766 7369
CHENEVERT/SODERBERG, Baton Rouge	504 291 7884
CLAUS & CLAUS, Baton Rouge	504 927 1982
CLEMENTS BLANCHARD HOLMES, Baton Rouge	504 292 2929
ROBERT COLEMAN, Baton Rouge	504 343 5870

CRUMP ASSOCIATES, Baton Rouge	504 291 9483
JOHN DESMOND & ASSOCIATES, Baton Rouge	504 387 3381
JAMES D. DODDS, Baton Rouge	504 927 1777
RAYMIE EDMONDS ARCHITECT, Baton Rouge	504 383 6439
W.J. EVANS ARCHITECT, Baton Rouge	504 383 7503
LOUIS H. FAXON, INC., Baton Rouge	504 387 0828
KEVIN LAWRENCE HARRIS, Baton Rouge	504 346 0724
KARL HARVEY ASSOCIATES, Baton Rouge	504 922 5115
HENDRICK GUTEKUNST & LEWIS, Baton Rouge	504 293 6363
HERSCHEL HOFFPAUIR, Baton Rouge	504 343 8731
ALDEN S. HOLLOWAY ARCHITECT, Baton Rouge	504 926 0050
C. DALE HOTARD ARCHITECT, Baton Rouge	504 925 2323
JAMES G. HOWELL, Baton Rouge	504 293 9592
HUGHES AND ASSOCIATES, Baton Rouge	504 922 9967
HUNT THURMAN ASSOCIATES, Baton Rouge	504 357 2649
CHARLES K. HUTCHINSON ARCHITECT, Baton Rouge	504 292 7413
DOUGLAS A. JONES ARCHITECT, Baton Rouge	504 925 0123
LASSEIGNE & LEGETT, Baton Rouge	504 926 1432
J. ELLIOTT LORMAND, Baton Rouge	504 766 3790
GREGORY P. MATHERINE, Baton Rouge	504 766 9744
MARK R. MONTGOMERY ARCHITECT, Baton Rouge	504 928 1163
NEWMAN & GRACE, Baton Rouge	504 292 1210
RAYMOND G. POST ARCHITECTS, Baton Rouge	504 293 6964
RONALD SAPP, Baton Rouge	504 346 0695
CHARLES E. SCHWING & ASSOCIATES, Baton Rouge	504 344 3000
SMITH & CHAMPAGNE, Baton Rouge	504 343 1705
STEWART KUYRKENDAL, Baton Rouge	504 925 2429
A. HAYS TOWN INC., Baton Rouge	504 766 4802
W. CONWAY WASHBURN ARCHITECT, Baton Rouge	504 928 2402
RUSSELL WASHER & ASSOCIATES, Baton Rouge	504 767 1530
JULIAN T. WHITE ARCHITECT, Baton Rouge	504 383 9534
WILLIAMSON CARROLL, Baton Rouge	504 383 7565
KNIGHT AND KOONCE, Bogalusa	504 735 1010
KELLY & DOUGHTY ARCHITECTS, Bossier	318 742 3351
HECK & CAREY, Chalmette	504 277 2919
FAUNTLEROY & LATHAM ARCHITECTS, Covington	504 893 4100
ARTHUR MIDDLETON III, Covington	504 892 3292
RYAN ARCHITECTS, Covington	504 892 6696
JAMES P. LABARRE, Denham Springs	504 664 1934
ALEX THERIOT JR. AND ASSOCIATES, Denham Springs	504 665 5173
HENRY L. CHAUVIN ARCHITECT, Gonzales	504 644 4595
BRADLEY MIREMONT BLEWSTER ARCHITECTS, Hammond	504 542 4138

GOSSEN & GASSAWAY, Hammond	504 345`5047
HOLLY AND SMITH, Hammond	504 345 5210
FRANCISCO ALECHA, Harahan	504 733 4336
HOUSTON J. LIRETTE JR. ARCHITECTS, Houma	504 851 1484
CURTIS J. MARCELLO ARCHITECT, Houma	504 876 3143
WHITNEY ASSOCIATES LTD., Houma	504 868 5020
EDMOND A. CHERAMIE ARCHITECT, LaRose	504 693 8000
A.O. ARCHITECTS, Lafayette	318 237 3300
ARCHITECTS SOUTHWEST, Lafayette	318 237 2211
BARRAS AND BREAUX ARCHITECTS, Lafayette	318 232 7840
BOURGEOIS PONTIFF ARCHITECTS, Lafayette	318 237 9200
DAN P. BRANCH, Lafayette	318 235 1890
BROUSSARD PECOT & ASSOCIATES, Lafayette	318 235 5004
CORNE SELLERS & ASSOCIATES, Lafayette	318 232 0773
JOHNSTONE ASSOCIATES, INC., Lafayette	318 235 5464
N. L. ARCHITECTS, Lafayette	318 237 6778
DON J. O'ROURKE & ASSOCIATES LTD., Lafayette	318 232 2838
FABIAN PATIN & ASSOCIATES, Lafayette	318 233 4103
PERKINS/GUIDRY/BEAZLEY/OSTTEEN, Lafayette	318 233 0614
SCHOEFFLER & IBOURDIER ARCHITECTS, Lafayette	318 237 1683
ARCHITECTURE SIX, Lake Charles	318 433 7352
CHAMPEAUX LANDRY INC., Lake Charles	318 439 8871
DUNN, QUINN, GALLAUGHER & QUINN, Lake Charles	318 436 4393
J.M. GABRIEL & ASSOCIATES, Lake Charles	318 433 2525
HACKETT & BAILEY, Lake Charles	318 478 1614
KLEINSCHMIDT & ASSOCIATES, Lake Charles	318 477 7755
C. GAYLE ZEMBOWER ARCHITECT INC., Lake Charles	318 477 7160
ALCIATORE ASSOCIATES, Metairie	504 888 2724
CHARLES COLBERT, Metairie	504 834 8151
RALPH J. DANSEREAU ARCHITECT, Metairie	504 834 4033
EHLINGER & ASSOCIATES INC., Metairie	504 455 8911
FAVROT AND SHANE, Metairie	504 885 4885
GRIMBALL GORRONDONA SAVOYE, Metairie	504 837 1255
GLENN C. HIGGINS ARCHITECT, Metairie	504 885 4363
LEVET & DAIGLE, Metairie	504 834 4777
N. Y. ARCHITECTS, Metairie	504 885 0500
C. E. MEYER & ASSOCIATES, Metairie	504 885 9892
L. DOW OLIVER & ASSOCIATES INC., Metairie	504 455 7965
PIQUE WEINSTEIN PIQUE, Metairie	504 835 8885
GERRARD RAYMOND ARCHITECT, Metairie	504 885 9590
STOFFLE ASSOCIATES, Metairie	504 835 7660
LAWRENCE TAFFARO & ASSOCIATES, Metairie	504 833 4543

TIMPA & ASSOCIATES, Metairie	504 885 6834
ARCHITECTURE PLUS, Monroe	318 387 2800
BERNARD L. BRYANT & ASSOCIATES, Monroe	318 388 2791
WILLIAM CAVITT COOKSTON, Monroe	318 387 7766
S. E. HUEY CO., Monroe	318 325 1791
ROY JOHNS ARCHITECT, Monroe	318 323 1766
HERBERT LAND ARCHITECTS, Monroe	318 325 6026
TRAVIS OLIVER III ARCHITECT, Monroe	318 387 4555
SPACE PLANNERS ARCHITECTS, Monroe	318 322 4183
DONALD E. WADLEY ARCHITECT, Monroe	318 388 4301
WELLS, PARKER & WALPOLE, Monroe	318 322 7148
FIRMIN ARCHITECTS LTD., Morgan City	504 384 3094
E. P. DOBSON ARCHITECT, Natchitoches	318 352 4922
HERMAN GESSER & ASSOCIATES, New Iberia	318 365 8166
MELVIN J. OUBRE ARCHITECT, New Iberia	318 369 9097
SEGURA BEYT AND ASSOCIATES, New Iberia	318 365 6678
ARGUS ARCHITECTS, New Orleans	504 945 8922
BIERY AND ASSOCIATES, New Orleans	504 523 6828
BONIE ASSOCIATES, New Orleans	504 488 0473
BETTY L. MOSS ARCHITECT, New Orleans	504 525 9901
ARCHITECTS SOUTH INC., New Orleans	504 522 5494
BILLES/MANNING ARCHITECTS, New Orleans	504 523 5366
BLITCH ARCHITECTS, New Orleans	504 524 4634
VICTOR BRUNO ARCHITECT, New Orleans	504 821 9900
BURGDAHL GRAVES, New Orleans	504 482 4433
HAROLD BURNS & ASSOCIATES, New Orleans	504 891 6349
CAMPO ASSOCIATES, New Orleans	504 568 9912
CIMINI MERIC BURNS COUNCE, New Orleans	504 588 9488
CONCORDIA ARCHITECTS, New Orleans	504 525 1862
NATHANIEL C. CURTIS, JR. ARCHITECTS, New Orleans	504 899 5622
ARTHUR Q. DAVIS & PARTNERS, New Orleans	504 566 0888
ESKEW VOGT SALVATO & FILSON, New Orleans	504 561 8686
FARNET ARCHITECTS, New Orleans	504 949 6000
BARRY FOX ASSOCIATES, New Orleans	504 897 6989
HEBEISEN & ASSOCIATES, INC., New Orleans	504 581 6409
IMRE HEGEIDUS & ASSOCIATED, New Orleans	504 522 6525
H. HERSHBERG & ASSOCIATES, New Orleans	504 522 9663
JAHNCKE SPOONER ASSOCIATES, New Orleans	504 899 6271
KESSELS DIBOLL KESSELS, New Orleans	504 522 8625
KOCH & WILSON, New Orleans	504 581 7023
LABOUISSE & WAGGONNER, New Orleans	504 524 5308
A.C. LEDNER & ASSOCIATES, New Orleans	504 488 6326

LYONS & HUDSON ARCHITECTS, New Orleans	504 525 4491
THE MATHES GROUP, New Orleans	504 586 9303
40/41 **E. EEAN McNAUGHTON ARCHITECTS, New Orleans**	**504 586 1870**
MORTON & ASSOCIATES, New Orleans	504 482 3183
MUSSO HAIZLIP ARCHITECTS, New Orleans	504 523 7979
OLIVIER ASSOCIATES, New Orleans	504 488 6438
OUBRE & ASSOCIATES, New Orleans	504 482 7839
LEONARD SALVATO, New Orleans	504 525 4995
I. WM. SIZELER & ASSOCIATES, New Orleans	504 523 6472
STEINMETZ & ASSOCIATES, New Orleans	504 523 6129
PETER M. TRAPOLIN & ASSOCIATES, New Orleans	504 523 2772
VERGES ASSOCIATES ARCHITECTS, New Orleans	504 488 7739
JOHN C. WILLIAMS ARCHITECTS, New Orleans	504 523 4609
YEATES & YEATES, New Orleans	504 522 7218
D'AVY & D'AVY ARCHITECTS, Opelousas	318 942 2678
GAUDET & TOLSON LTD., Opelousas	318 948 1202
HAMILTON & ASSOCIATES, Opelousas	318 948 8271
ADM ASSOCIATES, Ruston	318 255 0006
JOHN M. DOUGHERTY ARCHITECT, Ruston	318 255 3220
ANNAN & GILMER, Shreveport	318 222 9545
EMERSON & ASSOCIATES, Shreveport	318 869 1695
EVANS & EVANS, Shreveport	318 222 9497
HAAS & MASSEY, Shreveport	318 222 2872
GEORGE A. JACKSON, Shreveport	318 226 1454
RALPH KIPER ARCHITECT, Shreveport	318 222 7580
MORGAN, O'NEAL, HILL & SUTTON, Shreveport	318 221 1623
DAVID JAY NANCE, Shreveport	318 424 3274
NEWMAN PARTNERSHIP, Shreveport	318 424 8414
POLLARD & EBBING INC., Shreveport	318 798 7301
DARYL F. ROZELL ARCHITECT, Shreveport	318 861 7112
SCHULDT ASSOCIATES INC., Shreveport	318 226 1404
SHOEMAKER, COLBERT, BRODNAX, Shreveport	318 425 8649
SLACK BRADLEY MIREMONT & ASSOCIATES, Shreveport	318 425 3030
SOMDAL ASSOCIATES, Shreveport	318 425 7721
VENTURE ARCHITECTS, Shreveport	318 636 6659
WALKER & WALKER, Shreveport	318 425 8651
ROLAND A. ALPHA ARCHITECT, Slidell	504 649 7105
MERVIN L. JOHNSON ARCHITECT, Slidell	504 833 3433
ELLENDER BROUSSARD & ASSOCIATES, Sulphur	318 527 3603
VINCENT & KING, Sulphur	318 527 0781
FOURNET & FOURNET, Thibodaux	504 446 3078
GOSSEN GASSAWAY & ASSOCIATES LTD., Thibodaux	504 447 9229

RICHARD WEIMER & ASSOCIATES, Thibodaux	504 447 9043	LEWIS GRAEBER, Jackson	601 366 3611
BEUFORD G. JACKA ARCHITECT, West Monroe	318 325 6816	RALPH MAISEL, Jackson	601 362 9292
		MALVANEY ASSOCIATES, Jackson	601 353 5347
M I S S I S S I P P I		JOHN W. STAATS, Jackson	601 981 2442
HOPKINS ASSOCIATES, Biloxi	601 374 6611	ENOCH WILLIAMS, Jackson	601 355 8857
BARNES, COMISH, DEWEESE, Clarksdale	601 627 1163	PATRICK J. YOUNG, Jackson	601 956 4307
GODBOLD, DICKSON, Clarksdale	601 624 8531	DESIGN PROFESSIONAL, Madison	601 957 1948
SAMUEL KAYE, Columbus	601 327 6241	ARCHER AND ARCHER, Meridian	601 483 4873
VIRDEN, FIELDS, ALEXANDER, Columbus	601 328 7101	ASSOCIATED CONSULTANTS, Meridian	601 693 6156
HAROLD KAPLAN, Greenville	601 332 5472	McMULLAN/CLOPTON, Meridian	601 693 3453
LOWELL P. MILLS, Greenville	601 332 0388	ARNOLD J. AHO, Mississippi State	601 323 7121
OAKMAN HARVEY, ARCHITECTS, Greenville	601 378 8825	CHARLES MORONEY, Natchez	601 442 5791
VIRDEN FIELDS & ALEXANDER, Greenville	601 328 7101	DAVID PEABODY, Natchez	601 445 2180
BOWMAN & BOWMAN, Greenwood	601 453 7181	JOHNNY WAYCASTER, ARCHITECTS, Natchez	601 442 3649
McADAMS, Greenwood	601 453 6427	THOMAS A. HABEEB, Pascagoula	601 762 1101
McREE DARDAMAN JONES, Grenada	601 226 7115	SLAUGHTER & ALLRED, Pascagoula	601 762 1975
DUNN & RANDALL, Gulfport	601 896 1859	AC SMITH & ASSOCIATES, Pascagoula	601 769 8180
MICHAEL A. ELIZONDO, Gulfport	601 865 2943	TOMPKINS HANSEN & FIELDS, Pascagoula	601 769 5017
EQUITY INVESTMENTS, Gulfport	601 868 9199	J MYKOLYK AND ASSOCIATES, Pass Christian	601 452 7832
CHARLES L. PROFFER, Gulfport	601 863 6007	CLINGAN & ASSOCIATES, Ridgeland	601 856 6773
SHAW/WALKER, Gulfport	601 864 1202	CONSTRUCTION MANAGEMENT PLUS, Ridgeland	601 957 3363
STEPHEN BLAIR, Hattiesburg	601 544 0221	CHARLES D. LOPER, Ridgeland	601 856 5234
DAVID K. HEMETER, ARCHITECT, Hattiesburg	601 544 4741	TERENCE O. YOUNG, ARCHITECT, Senatobia	601 562 5332
LANDRY ASSOCIATES, Hattiesburg	601 544 2020	THOMAS SHELTON JONES & ASSOCIATES, Starkville	601 323 3762
DAVID SHELEY, Hattiesburg	601 582 4249	GARY SHAFER, Starkville	601 323 1628
BARLOW & PLUNKETT, Jackson	601 352 8377	WAKEMAN & ASSOCIATES, Starkville	601 323 4425
BARRON & POLK, Jackson	601 352 7878	WENZEL & ASSOCIATES, Tunica	601 363 1811
BENNETT/TIMMER, Jackson	601 956 8503	JOHNSON ASSOCIATES, P.A., Tupelo	601 844 1822
CANIZARO TRIGIANI, Jackson	601 948 7337	McCARTY ARCHITECTS, Tupelo	601 844 4400
CLEMMER & CLARK, Jackson	601 948 4145	A.J. STAUB III & ASSOCIATES, Tupelo	601 844 5843
COOKE DOUGLAS FARR LTD., Jackson	601 366 3110	S.J. TUMINELLO ARCHITECTS, Vicksburg	601 636 0033
WALTER COOPER, Jackson	601 981 2108	PRYOR & MORROW, West Point	601 494 1047
CRAIG, SIMMONS, SINGLETON, Jackson	601 981 2363		
DEAN/DALE & DEAN, Jackson	601 939 7717	**N O R T H C A R O L I N A**	
GODFREY, BASSETT & KUYKENDALL, Jackson	601 373 4552	HAWTHORNE ENTERPRISES, Aberdeen	919 944 2771
HARRY HAAS, Jackson	601 362 7745	SURAPON SUJJAVANICH, Apex	919 362 0470
ROBERT V. M. HARRISON, Jackson	601 362 4899	LARRY E. AUSTIN, Asheboro	919 672 1469
HESTER AND ASSOCIATES, Jackson	601 948 8803	BOONE HUNTON ASSOCIATES, Asheville	704 645 7195
JH & J LTD/ARCHITECTS, Jackson	601 948 4601	JOHN S. ELLIS, Asheville	704 989 9296
WILLIAM P. JOSEPH, Jackson	601 352 1100	R.S. GRIFFIN, Asheville	704 274 5979
JAMES C. LEE & ASSOCIATES, Jackson	601 982 4153	DANIE A. JOHNSON, Asheville	704 252 9649
THE LEWIS PARTNERSHIP, Jackson	601 982 4375	J BERTRAM KING, Asheville	704 252 6782

PADGETT & FREEMAN, Asheville	704 254 1963	
WALLACE PATERSON, Asheville	704 254 2190	
ROGERS/DAMERON, Asheville	704 258 8755	
SPACEPLAN/ARCHITECTURE, Asheville	704 252 9649	
T. EDMUND WHITMIRE, Asheville	704 254 9100	
JAN M. WIEGMAN, Asheville	704 255 7684	
WOOD AND CORT, Asheville	704 252 3513	
WOODARD AND ROBERTS, Asheville	704 254 8363	
HOWELL ASSOCIATES, Blowing Rock	704 264 5583	
RAYMOND HOWELL, Boone	704 264 5583	
DANIELS & WORLEY, Brevard	704 884 2552	
McDONALD & BREWTON, Brevard	704 883 9255	
ALLEY, WILLIAMS, CARMEN, Burlington	919 226 5534	
VERNON E. LEWIS, Burlington	919 226 6007	
G. CLEVELAND PATE, Cary	919 469 0968	
PETERSON ASSOCIATES, Cary	919 481 0666	
SEARS, HACKNEY, SMITH, KEENEK, Cary	919 467 5703	
JAMES HUNTER MITCHELL, Cashiers	704 743 2968	
JERRY W. HAGER, Catawba	704 241 3228	
20 LUCY CAROL DAVIS ASSOCIATES, Chapel Hill	**919 933 7775**	
DALE DIXON AND ASSOCIATES, Chapel Hill	919 968 8333	
LEHMANN MEHLER ARCHITECTS, Chapel Hill	919 933 3711	
AA PELOQUIN, Chapel Hill	919 929 5450	
J. KNOX TATE, Chapel Hill	919 967 9678	
JAMES M. WEBB, Chapel Hill	919 929 6385	
L. SUMNER WINN JR., Chapel Hill	919 942 7007	
ABERNETHY POETZSCH, Charlotte	704 372 1860	
ADEP, P.A., Charlotte	704 375 6038	
KENNETH ANDREWS, Charlotte	704 547 1505	
PAUL BRASWELL, Charlotte	704 332 2951	
CAMAS ASSOCIATES, Charlotte	704 372 0491	
CARY, MARTIN McMULLEN, Charlotte	704 527 5123	
CLARK TRIBBLE HARRIS, Charlotte	704 333 6686	
W CRUTCHER ROSS ASSOCIATES, Charlotte	704 333 1291	
18/19 DALTON MORAN SHOOK, ARCHITECTURE, INC., Charlotte	**704 372 0116**	
DELLINGER LEE ASSOCIATES, Charlotte	704 332 2446	
DAVID F. FURMAN, Charlotte	704 332 2942	
FWA GROUP, Charlotte	704 332 7004	
GODWIN ASSOCIATES, Charlotte	704 377 4051	
GRIER, FRIPP ASSOCIATES, Charlotte	704 527 2514	
GUNN HARDAWAY, Charlotte	704 377 8800	
HARWOOD BEEBE/BOB JOHNSON, Charlotte	704 372 0070	

HAWKINS KIBLER ASSOCIATES, Charlotte	704 376 3561
HODGE AHEARN, Charlotte	704 525 5423
GANTT HUBERMAN, Charlotte	704 334 6436
JOHN KNIGHT, Charlotte	704 377 4385
LITTLE & ASSOCIATES, Charlotte	704 525 6350
CHARLES T. MAIN, INC., Charlotte	704 529 6246
McCULLOCH ENGLAND ASSOCIATES, Charlotte	704 372 2740
MIDDLETON, McMILLAN, Charlotte	704 364 8660
BRICE MORRIS ASSOCIATES, Charlotte	704 334 7339
ODELL ASSOCIATES, Charlotte	704 377 5941
OGBURN & STEVER, Charlotte	704 333 0101
ORKAN ARCHITECTURE, Charlotte	704 527 5555
OVERCASH & HARRIS, Charlotte	704 375 1615
JN PEASE ASSOCIATES, Charlotte	704 376 6423
PETERSON ASSOCIATES, Charlotte	704 357 3322
SURRATT, SMITH, ABERNATHY, Charlotte	704 357 1000
HAL TRIBBLE, Charlotte	704 333 7907
WHEATLEY, WILLIAMS, Charlotte	704 375 3425
MURRAY WHISNANT, Charlotte	704 375 2788
WILBER, KENDRICK, WORKMAN, Charlotte	704 535 2582
WOOLPERT CONSULTANTS, Charlotte	704 525 6284
ROBERT W. CARR, Durham	919 688 6308
DEPASQUALE, THOMPSON, Durham	919 688 8102
DOUGLAS E. GRIFFIN, Durham	919 383 7817
HARRIS & PYNE, Durham	919 688 7351
SAMUEL HODGES, Durham	919 682 0379
MAX ISLEY, Durham	919 489 7417
ROMAN KOLODIJ, Durham	919 286 7398
JOHN D. LATIMER & ASSOCIATES, Durham	919 489 3311
NICHOLSON ASSOCIATES, Durham	919 682 9264
SUN FOREST INC., Durham	919 361 9888
JOSEPH H. YONGUE, Durham	919 544 0145
RALPH J. AUSTIN, Eden	919 623 9631
JACK McM. PRUDEN, Edenton	919 482 2340
NOEL N. COLTRANE JR., Elizabeth City	919 338 3660
HICKS ARCHITECTS, Fayetteville	919 323 3911
LSV, Fayetteville	919 485 4108
MacMILLAN & MacMILLAN, Fayetteville	919 483 2710
ROBERT N. SHULLER, Fayetteville	919 484 4989
RE SMITH, Fuquay-Varina	919 552 4011
BEAN & YEARGIN, Gastonia	704 864 4508
CURRY DESIGN GROUP, Gastonia	704 866 9120

STEWART & COOPER, Gastonia	919 868 6311	PINEHURST ENTERPRISES, Pinehurst	919 295 5720
AEP COLLABORATIVE, Greensboro	919 272 0202	A E C, Pineville	704 332 4658
ALFRED C. DAVID, Greensboro	919 275 3907	ALPHA DESIGN, Raleigh	919 833 3631
G. DONALD DUDLEY, Greensboro	919 378 9311	B & V ENGINEERS, Raleigh	919 851 0500
MARIO GRIGNI, Greensboro	919 288 9891	BALLARD, McCREDIE, ELLIOTT, Raleigh	919 872 6100
ROBERT A. HAHN, Greensboro	919 292 7578	BEST AND ASSOCIATES, Raleigh	919 787 4623
J. HYATT HAMMOND, Greensboro	919 370 8400	BOISSEAU DESIGN, Raleigh	919 847 5860
CARL P. MYATT, Greensboro	919 274 3554	JAMES C. BUIE, Raleigh	919 781 4873
MAJOR S. SANDERS, Greensboro	919 274 2622	CLEARSCAPES, Raleigh	919 821 2775
STEC AND COMPANY, Greensboro	919 275 5371	WALTER DAVIS, Raleigh	919 881 0404
DUDLEY & SHOE, Greenville	919 758 3138	DEWBERRY & DAVIS, Raleigh	919 847 0418
DAVID LEROY PARROTT, Henderson	919 722 2679	DOGGETT ARCHITECTS, Raleigh	919 847 2122
JAMES M. STEVENSON, Henderson	919 492 5330	DW WOLFE AND ASSOCIATES, Raleigh	919 876 9217
ALLEN J. BOLICK, Hickory	704 324 7056	ELLINWOOD DESIGN, Raleigh	919 781 1083
CLEMMER BUSH SILLS, Hickory	704 322 3403	ENVIROTEK, INC., Raleigh	919 832 6658
BEEMER HARRELL, Hickory	704 322 3125	FISHER & TAYLOR, Raleigh	919 782 3729
JAMES N. SHERRILL, Hickory	704 322 9077	HAGER, SMITH & HUFFMAN, Raleigh	919 821 5547
JOHN K. ANDERSON, High Point	919 882 0163	HALLOWAY REEVES ARCHITECTS, Raleigh	919 834 0304
C. MICHAEL AUSTIN, High Point	919 454 1944	HASKINS AND RICE, Raleigh	919 787 9751
WILLIAM F. FREEMAN JR., High Point	919 885 4031	INNOVATION DESIGN, Raleigh	919 832 6303
GARY D. HAYNES, High Point	919 889 2467	JENKINS & HALE, Raleigh	919 856 0856
DAVID B. ODEN, High Point	919 883 6414	JOHN BOWLES KNOX, Raleigh	919 781 8582
SMITHEY & BOYNTON, High Point	919 884 1225	LELAND/GONZALEZ, Raleigh	919 833 6439
NORMAN L. ZIMMERMAN, High Point	919 869 3515	MACE & ASSOCIATES, Raleigh	919 787 1984
DeWOLF ASSOCIATES, Highlands	704 526 3923	McKIMMON/EDWARDS/HITCH, Raleigh	919 782 2272
JOHN C. WILLIAMS JR., Hillsborough	919 732 6811	MEG McLAURIN, Raleigh	919 832 5744
THEODORE PETERS, Jacksonville	919 455 0015	MOORE & BURTON, Raleigh	919 782 6471
ARCHITECTURAL BUILDING CONSULTANTS, Kill Devil Hills	919 441 1410	OPUN ONE ARCHITECTURE, Raleigh	919 834 9441
JAMES R. McVICKER JR., Laurinburg	919 276 2313	PDA, Raleigh	919 821 0505
SAM T. SNOWDON JR., Laurinburg	919 276 2618	QUICK ASSOCIATES, Raleigh	919 781 0375
THOMPSON AND McVICKER, Lumberton	919 739 0861	RAMSAY ASSOCIATES, Raleigh	919 781 0026
PERIGON, Matthews	704 847 6346	SCOVIL & RAIRDEN, Raleigh	919 876 1048
FRANK M. WILLIAMS, Matthews	704 847 9851	SHAWCROFT TAYLOR, Raleigh	919 781 0015
M. DEAN BASKINS, Monroe	704 289 4028	MILTON SMALL, Raleigh	919 833 1994
JOHN H. DICKERSON, Monroe	704 283 8268	GEORGE SMART INC., Raleigh	919 834 8488
CECIL HODGE, Monroe	704 283 2908	THE TAYNTON ARCHITECTURAL PRACTICE, Raleigh	919 838 9159
M Y FOLGER & ASSOCIATES, Morganton	704 437 3411	WILLIAM WAKEHAM, Raleigh	919 787 3595
ROBERT B. SALSBURY, Morganton	704 437 2504	F. CARTER WILLIAMS, Raleigh	919 833 2536
APPLEGATE ARCHITECTS, New Bern	919 633 5603	O´BRIEN ATKINS ASSOCIATES, Research Triangle Park	919 941 9000
PETERSON ARCHITECTS, New Bern	919 637 6783	DOVE & KNIGHT, Rocky Mount	919 443 3173
STEPHENS & FRANCIS, New Bern	919 637 3301	JAMES F. DUGAN III, Rocky Mount	919 446 5319
SMITH & REINHARDT, Newton	704 464 2086	RYLAND P. EDWARDS, Rocky Mount	919 443 9220

C. ROBERT SHIELDS, Rocky Mount	919 977 3227
ERROL JORDAN WARREN JR., Rocky Mount	919 977 7787
RAMSAY & ASSOCIATES, Salisbury	704 633 3121
ROBERT F. STONE, Salisbury	704 633 1874
ARCHITECTURE INC., Sanford	919 774 4811
MULLINS & SHERMAN, Sanford	919 775 2355
ARCHITECTURAL DESIGN, Shelby	704 482 6755
HOLLAND AND HAMRICK, Shelby	704 487 8578
MARTIN, BARDSLEY & ANTHONY, Shelby	704 484 0264
HAYES & HOWELL, Southern Pines	919 692 7316
PHILLIPS AND ASSOCIATES, Southern Pines	919 944 7206
STUART/FITCHETT, Southern Pines	919 692 8570
RICHARD L. ANDREWS, Tarboro	919 823 7335
HOLLAND BRADY JR., Tryon	704 859 6006
WILSON ARCHITECTURE, Washington	919 946 6532
FOY & LEE, Waynesville	704 456 7363
BREWSTER WARD, Waynesville	704 452 4448
TASHIRO ASSOCIATES, Wilkesboro	919 838 2732
BALLARD, McKIM & SAWYER, Wilmington	919 762 2621
BONEY ARCHITECTS, Wilmington	919 763 9901
RANDALL BRAY, Wilmington	919 762 0710
LIGON FLYNN, Wilmington	919 343 0660
JEFFERIES & FARIS, Wilmington	919 762 3371
HENRY W. JOHNSTON, Wilmington	919 762 5739
JOHN R. OXENFELD, Wilmington	919 763 3381
JOHN SAWYER, Wilmington	919 762 0892
SKINNER, LAMM, HOOD & HIGHSMITH, Wilson	919 291 4127
EDWIN E. BOULDIN JR., Winston-Salem	919 725 5386
FRED W. BUTNER JR., Winston-Salem	919 725 5394
CALLOWAY JOHNSON, Winston-Salem	919 724 1503
CUNDIFF ASSOCIATES, Winston-Salem	919 725 2748
HAMMILL/WALTER, Winston-Salem	919 725 1371
HINES, NORTHUP, ERSOY, Winston-Salem	919 725 1361
THOMAS H. HUGHES & ASSOCIATES, Winston-Salem	919 722 4447
KIRBY ASSOCIATES, Winston-Salem	919 723 6706
NEWMAN & JONES, Winston-Salem	919 725 1346
TROXELL ASSOCIATES, Winston-Salem	919 723 4371
JC WOODALL, Winston-Salem	919 724 0950
SYNTHESIS INC., Wrightsville Beach	919 256 4141

N E W   J E R S E Y

28/29 **MICHAEL GRAVES ARCHITECT, Princeton**	**609 924 6409**

N E W   Y O R K

12/13 **JOHN BURGEE ARCHITECTS, New York**	**212 751 7440**
36/37 **KOHN PEDERSON FOX ASSOCIATES, New York**	**212 977 6500**
50/51 **PEI, COBB, FREED & PARTNERS, New York**	**212 751 3122**

O K L A H O M A

JOE ANDRASH, Oklahoma City	405 848 6809
BAUMEISTER MANKIN, Oklahoma City	405 525 8451
LOFTIS DOWNING LADREW, Oklahoma City	405 232 3232
MILES & ASSOCIATES, Oklahoma City	405 235 3915
T.A.P., Oklahoma City	405 232 8787
BOYD GROUP, Tulsa	918 622 3324
COOK ASSOCIATES, Tulsa	918 494 6700
TURNER & ASSOCIATES, Tulsa	918 582 2282
WOZENCRAFT/MOWERY/HAWKINS, Tulsa	918 663 2006

P U E R T O   R I C O

WILLIAM MARTINEZ ROIG, Guaynabo	809 789 2429
WILLIAM M. BALBI, Hato Rey	809 754 0078
TORRES GAZTAMBIDE, Hato Rey	809 753 1223
INTERPLAN, PUERTO RICO, Hato Rey	809 753 0539
GEORGE Z. MARK, Hato Rey	809 754 7840
ARQUITECTURA R D OLABARRIETA, Hato Rey	809 753 8116
RODRIGUES, FLORES, Hato Rey	809 764 7135
SAMUEL CORCHADO VEGA, Hato Rey	809 751 6676
MAX A. CHOW & ASSOCIATES, Old San Juan	809 721 7963
JORGE DEL RIO, Rio Piedras	809 765 3720
McCLINTOCK ASSOCIATES, Rio Piedras	809 754 7745
GUILLERMO ALVEREZ MENOCAL, Rio Piedras	809 765 0116
MOLINARI ARCHITECTS, San Juan	809 793 3950
DR. FERNANDO ABRUNA, San Juan	809 724 0987
RENE ACOSTA, San Juan	809 763 3212
AGRAIT, BERMUDEZ, BETANCOURT, San Juan	809 753 1223
ARCHICORPS, San Juan	809 721 6956
ARCHITECTURAL AFFILIATES, San Juan	809 763 1313
CAPACETE, MARTIN, San Juan	809 782 4144
JRC DAVIS PAGAN, San Juan	809 721 3700
MARK M. FAUGENBLAT & ASSOCIATES, San Juan	809 753 0539
JOSE M. GARCIA GOMEZ, San Juan	809 725 6762
HERNANDEZ VEGA Y BAUZA, San Juan	809 751 7241
THE OFFICE OF HENRY KLUMB, San Juan	809 763 4340
MENDEZ, BRUNNER & ASSOCIATES, San Juan	809 721 3900

EVELIO O. PINA, San Juan — 809 722 0970

RAUL RIVERA ORTIZ, San Juan — 809 728 7009

EDWARD UNDERWOOD RIOS, San Juan — 809 766 1305

UNIPRO: ARCHITECTS, San Juan — 809 783 0085

JULIO WRIGHT, San Juan — 809 731 6100

YANEZ & ARCHILIA, San Juan — 809 781 1092

AYBAR IMBERT & RIVIERA, Santurce — 809 753 7616

LUIS FLORES, Santurce — 809 725 8787

FRACINETTI ARQUITECTOS, Santurce — 809 724 1411

ARTURO J. GARCIA, Santurce — 809 723 3082

GUTIERREZ & GUTIERREZ, Santurce — 809 766 0566

JIMENEZ AND RODRIGUEZ-BARCELO, Santurce — 809 721 0055

TORRES MARVEL FLORES, Santurce — 809 725 8787

PABLO QUINONES, Santurce — 809 726 0951

CARLOS R. SANZ, Santurce — 809 792 5732

SOLER CLOQUELL, Santurce — 809 723 1894

TORO FERRER AND ASSOCIATES, Santurce — 809 721 3700

SOUTH CAROLINA

HOLLAND ARCHITECTS, Aiken — 803 649 7020

H. M. MOORMANN, Aiken — 803 648 6833

WELLS, LAW & ASSOCIATES, Aiken — 803 648 9612

F.J. CLARK, INC., Anderson — 803 224 1661

FANT & FANT, Anderson — 803 226 6171

LONNIE WATT & ASSOCIATES, Anderson — 803 225 8225

MILTON WHITE, Anderson — 803 225 7211

FREDERICK & FREDERICK, Beaufort — 803 522 8422

THOMAS & DENZINGER, Beaufort — 803 524 6361

HENRY D. BOYKIN, Camden — 803 432 3233

ARCHITECTURAL CONCEPTS, Cayce — 803 796 9359

DAVID J. ALLISON, Charleston — 803 722 6111

BOHM, NBBJ, Charleston — 803 577 2163 .

O. DOUGLAS BOYCE, Charleston — 803 577 9949

CLARK & MENEFEE ARCHITECTS, Charleston — 803 226 6201

CONSTANTINE & CONSTANTINE, Charleston — 803 723 7244

CUMMINGS & McCRADY, Charleston — 803 577 5063

MARSHALL M. DRIVER & ASSOCIATES, Charleston — 803 762 2333

EVANS & SCHMIDT, Charleston — 803 723 5495

GALE ARCHITECTURAL, Charleston — 803 723 6538

J. HARRELL GANDY ARCHITECT, Charleston — 803 795 3464

GLICK/BOEHM, Charleston — 803 577 6377

GOTTSHALK ARCHITECTS, Charleston — 803 722 3103

GRIFFITH & KEYES ARCHITECTS, Charleston — 803 722 4100

GEORGE C. LEE, Charleston — 803 571 2526

LIOLLIO ASSOCIATES, Charleston — 803 556 6200

Ls3P, Charleston — 803 577 4444

MITCHELL/SMALL/DONAHUE & LOGAN, Charleston — 803 723 3407

EDWARD PINCKNY ASSOCIATES, Charleston — 803 723 9596

GEORGE PORCHER, ARCHITECT, INC., Charleston — 803 577 0410

WILLIAM RIESBERG, Charleston — 803 577 3431

ROSENBLUM & ASSOCIATES, Charleston — 803 577 6073

STEPHEN A. RUSSELL, ARCHITECT, Charleston — 803 577 3008

CHRIS SCHMITT & ASSOCIATES, Charleston — 803 795 4415

MICHAEL SPIVEY, Charleston — 803 795 9370

TYNES ASSOCIATES, Charleston — 803 767 0543

W. W. WARLICK ARCHITECTS, Charleston — 803 723 2316

ARCH I, Clemson — 803 654 7348

PETER KNOWLAND, Clemson — 803 654 6409

AEA, INC., Columbia — 803 256 8052

ANDERSON ASSOCIATES, Columbia — 803 254 8788

ARCHITRAVE, Columbia — 803 252 6636

BLUME, CANNON & OTT, Columbia — 803 771 4706

ARCHITECTS BOUDREAUX, Columbia — 803 799 0247

CALIFF AVENT ARCHITECTS, INC., Columbia — 803 256 1221

CARLISLE ASSOCIATES, Columbia — 803 252 3232

CARSON ASSOCIATES, INC., Columbia — 803 252 6106

CATALYST ARCHITECTS, Columbia — 803 254 9001

COLUMBIA ARCHITECTURAL GROUP, Columbia — 803 794 5780

COMPREHENSIVE ARCHITECTS, Columbia — 803 254 5050

CURT DAVIS & ASSOCIATES, Columbia — 803 799 6502

DESIGN COLLABORATIVE, INC., Columbia — 803 782 4488

AL FARNSWORTH, Columbia — 803 787 8894

FULMER & ASSOCIATES, Columbia — 803 252 4585

GMK HEALTH CARE INC., Columbia — 803 254 5473

HARMON & KEENAN, ARCHITECTS, Columbia — 803 787 7854

HEYWARD & ASSOCIATES, Columbia — 803 771 4254

JAMES ASSOCIATES ARCHITECTURAL CORP., Columbia — 803 252 6150

JENKINS, HANCOCK & SIDES, Columbia — 803 252 2400

JMBW & ASSOCIATES, Columbia — 803 799 6526

LAMBERT TATE ARCHITECTURE, Columbia — 803 799 5181

THE LPA GROUP, INC., Columbia — 803 254 2211

McCLAM/BLAKE ARCHITECTS, Columbia — 803 256 0356

W. POWERS McELVEEN AND ASSOCIATES, Columbia — 803 256 4121

McGEE-MEYER AND ASSOCIATES, Columbia — 803 799 7100

McNAIR, JOHNSON & ASSOCIATES, Columbia	803 799 5472	PELHAM ARCHITECTS, Greenville	803 271 7633
MOLTEN & LAMAR, Columbia	803 771 7008	JAMES E. PHILLIPS, Greenville	803 235 2305
SAFKO PROBST ARCHITECTS, P.A., Columbia	803 799 6786	THE PIEDMONT GROUP, Greenville	803 242 1717
WILBUR SMITH & ASSOCIATES, Columbia	803 738 0580	JUDITH POWELL DESIGN CONSULTANT, Greenville	803 235 0137
CARL JEFF STROUD, Columbia	803 736 1624	THE TARLETON TANKERSLEY GROUP, Greenville	803 235 1611
STUDIO INDIGO, Columbia	803 254 1224	TOWNSEND ARCHITECTURAL PLANNING, Greenville	803 271 7678
WITT & ASSOCIATES, Columbia	803 799 8991	TRIAD DESIGN GROUP, INC., Greenville	803 233 2721
JOHN L. BOURNE, Conway	803 248 2242	WELLS ASSOCIATES ARCHITECTS, Greenville	803 292 2802
RON REAGAN/ARCHITECT, Easley	803 855 3356	WESTBURY & ASSOCIATES, Greenville	803 233 2440
JAMES P. BARNES, Florence	803 669 0014	McKAY ZORN ASSOCIATES, Greenville	803 242 9719
J. MICHAEL De RIENZO, Florence	803 662 7651	DORN & STEVENSON, Greenwood	803 229 2100
DOWIS ASSOCIATES, Florence	803 669 5223	CLARK AND McCALL, Hartsville	803 332 7443
MUNFORD G. FULLER, Florence	803 662 9961	ROBERT H. GOODSON, Hartsville	803 383 5212
KEY ARCHITECTURE, Florence	803 665 6646	BESTE & ASSOCIATES, Hilton Head	803 842 8700
WILKINS/WOOD & ASSOCIATES, Florence	803 669 8266	W. S. CARSON, ARCHITECT, Hilton Head	803 681 2494
PETEET COMPANY, Georgetown	803 546 3812	ROBERT H. CHRISTIAN, ARCHITECT, Hilton Head	803 785 2376
W. BARRY AGNEW ARCHITECT, INC., Greenville	803 242 2514	CORKERN & ASSOCIATES, INC., Hilton Head	803 785 4236
ARD-WOOD, Greenville	803 242 5450	DOLPHIN CORPORATION, Hilton Head	803 785 6600
BARRY A. BANKES, Greenville	803 235 3449	EAST COAST ARCHITECTS, Hilton Head	803 681 8005
BROWNING, McCLAIN, Greenville	803 271 6403	GROUP III ARCHITECT, Hilton Head	803 842 3766
CRAIG GAULDEN & DAVIS ARCHITECTS, Greenville	803 242 0761	JOSEPH K. HALL, ARCHITECTS, Hilton Head	803 842 2936
CRS SIRRINE, Greenville	803 298 6000	HERMAN & GORDON ARCHITECTS, Hilton Head	803 785 5651
FLUOR DANIEL, Greenville	803 298 2500	KEANE ROBINSON ARCHITECTS. INC, Hilton Head	803 686 2020
DESIGN PARTNERSHIP, INC., Greenville	803 232 8200	McGINTY ASSOCIATES, Hilton Head	803 785 4265
DESIGNTEK, Greenville	803 246 6406	MINSON ARCHITECTS & PLANNERS, Hilton Head	803 785 2111
EASON, EARL & ASSOCIATES, Greenville	803 233 0053	THE VENABLE GROUP, Hilton Head	803 681 8424
THE ELLIS GROUP, Greenville	803 235 7464	WIGGINS AND ASSOCIATES, Hilton Head	803 785 5376
ENWRIGHT ASSOCIATES, INC., Greenville	803 232 8140	ARCHIPELAGOS, Hilton Head Island	803 785 9192
FREEMAN, WELLS & MAJOR, ARCHITECTS, Greenville	803 233 1642	JOHNSON PARTNERSHIP, Hilton Head Island	803 785 4666
MARK B. GARBER & ASSOCIATES, Greenville	803 299 7856	LEE McCLESKEY AND MILLER, Hilton Head Island	803 785 5171
DONALD A. GARDNER, Greenville	803 288 7850	T. PRITCHARD SMITH, Hilton Head Island	803 785 4098
W. E. GILBERT & ASSOCIATES, Greenville	803 297 9281	GERTRAUDE M. DILLING, Isle of Palms	803 886 6638
GREENE & ASSOCIATES, Greenville	803 232 7381	DAVID J. SHAW, Johns Island	803 768 0515
HARVLEY ASSOCIATES, Greenville	803 233 1120	BATES ASSOCIATES, Kiawah Island	803 768 5500
KAUFMAN ASSOCIATES, Greenville	803 299 0174	CARL BERRY, ARCHITECTURE, Mt. Pleasant	803 844 1105
KEITH ARCHITECTS, Greenville	803 235 2306	BURRESS OSMENT, Mt. Pleasant	803 884 6973
M.W.B. & COMPANY, Greenville	803 246 4582	J. E. GARDNER & ASSOCIATES, Mt. Pleasant	803 884 7242
J. HAROLD MACK & ASSOCIATES, Greenville	803 235 6342	McKELLAR BELL ASSOCIATES INC., Mt. Pleasant	803 844 9085
MILLER PLAYER & ASSOCIATES, Greenville	803 243 0177	R. NELSON CROWE, ARCHITECTS, Myrtle Beach	803 448 7700
NARRAMORE ASSOCIATES, INC., Greenville	803 242 9881	DESIGN INC., Myrtle Beach	803 236 3114
NEAL, PRINCE & PARTNERS, Greenville	803 235 0405	LAWSON, CONNOR & POTTER, Myrtle Beach	803 626 7436
ODELL ASSOCIATES, INC., Greenville	803 235 6600	MULLINAX WASH, Myrtle Beach	803 272 3397

PECRAM & ASSOCIATES, INC., Myrtle Beach	803 449 5302
TIMBES/WILUND/USRY, Myrtle Beach	803 449 5204
VGR ARCHITECTS, N. Augusta	803 379 8367
ARCHITECTURAL ASSOCIATES, Orangeburg	803 534 8585
SUMMERS & GARDNER, ARCHITECTS, Orangeburg	803 536 0035
S. GOGGANS & ASSOCIATES, INC., Pawleys Island	803 337 3431
GRAHAM/CARTER/AYRES, ARCHITECTS, Pawleys Island	803 337 3488
D. DWAYNE VERNON, Pawleys Island	803 337 3783
JOHN B. LANGLEY, Pendleton	803 646 7889
PENDLETON DESIGN GROUP, Pendleton	803 646 7866
SADLER & KENT, INC., Rock Hill	803 327 1171
ARCHITECTURE INCORPORATED, Spartanburg	803 582 7110
OLIVER K. CECIL, Spartanburg	803 583 7503
HOLLIS & CROCKER, Spartanburg	803 582 5269
JOLLY DERRICK AND ASSOCIATES, Spartanburg	803 582 1510
LOCKWOOD GREENE ENGINEERS, INC., Spartanburg	803 587 2000
McMILLAN & SATTERFIELD, Spartanburg	803 583 7480
O'CAIN, GILMORE & SMITH, Spartanburg	803 583 7275
THOMAS CAMPBELL PRIDGEON, INC., Spartanburg	803 583 1456
WESTMORELAND, McGARITY, PITTS, Spartanburg	803 582 2929
GRAGG & ASSOCIATES, INC., Summerville	803 875 4298
ANDERSON ARCHITECTS, Sumter	803 773 7019
DEMOSTHENES & McCREIGHT LTD., Sumter	803 773 3211
DESIGNTEC, P.A., Sumter	803 773 2700
DRAKEFORD JACKSON & ASSOCIATES, Sumter	803 773 4328
JAMES/DURANT/MATTHEWS/SHELLY, Sumter	803 773 3318
BEN G. COMPTON, ARCHITECT, West Columbia	803 791 5350
DRAFTS & JUMPER, ARCHITECTS, West Columbia	803 791 1020

TENNESSEE

WILLIAM D. PRICE, Blountville	615 323 4433
KARKAU & ASSOCIATES, Brentwood	615 340 6262
THOMAS & MILLER, Brentwood	615 377 9773
GUY GILLIAM, Briston	615 764 8322
PAT BALES & ASSOCIATES, Chattanooga	615 622 4146
DERTHICK, HENLEY & WILKERSON, Chattanooga	615 266 4816
HARRISON GILL, Chattanooga	615 622 1124
CHARLES KING, Chattanooga	615 267 2464
KLAUS PETER NENTWIG, Chattanooga	615 821 7569
NINO PICCOLO, Chattanooga	615 756 1320
SOCRATES S. SABATER, Chattanooga	615 622 5121
SELMON T. FRANKLIN, Chattanooga	615 266 1207

THE WAMP ALLIANCE, Chattanooga	615 267 9267
RUFUS JOHNSON, Clarksville	615 647 6301
STACKER, COOK, Clarksville	615 552 9149
VIOLETTE ARCHITECTURE, Clarksville	615 552 6878
SMITH DESIGN GROUP, Cleveland	615 472 5039
BREWER FIRM ARCHITECTS, Cordova	901 756 2807
ROBERT S. GOFORTH, Cordova	901 754 7757
UPLAND DESIGN GROUP, Crossville	615 484 7541
REEDY AND SYKES, Elizabethton	615 543 4781
DESIGN ASSOCIATES INC., Germantown	901 755 7180
MARY COATS, Jackson	901 423 1903
WILLIAM C. HARRIS, Jackson	901 427 8476
HART/FREELAND/ROBERTS, Jackson	901 668 8063
ABERNETHY ROBINSON McGAHEY, Johnson City	615 928 8286
BEESON, LUSK & STREET, Johnson City	615 928 1175
BEACH ASSOCIATES, Kingsport	615 247 9221
ALLEN N. DRYDEN, Kingsport	615 246 7761
DAVID LEONARD, Kingsport	615 246 7434
RENTENBACH & WRIGHT, Kingsport	615 378 4121
GEORGE ALLAN, Knoxville	615 637 7402
ARCHITECTS PLUS, Knoxville	615 546 8252
ARCHITECTURAL TECHNIQUES, Knoxville	615 584 7192
BARBER & McMURRAY, Knoxville	615 546 7441
BULLOCK SMITH & PARTNERS, Knoxville	615 546 5772
COMMUNITY TECTONICS, Knoxville	615 637 0890
DEWITT DYKES & ASSOCIATES, Knoxville	615 522 0018
DAVIS DOLLAR & ASSOCIATES, Knoxville	615 546 9374
ED GREEN AND ASSOCIATES, Knoxville	615 637 2341
GRIEVE & RUTH ARCHITECTS, Knoxville	615 637 0382
GSCD INC., Knoxville	615 546 7010
GUAY AND ASSOCIATES, Knoxville	615 546 1880
BUD HESTER, Knoxville	615 523 7105
KAATZ & BINKLEY, Knoxville	615 637 4156
LINDSAY & MAPLES, Knoxville	615 524 8684
MARTELLA ASSOCIATES, Knoxville	615 525 2556
McCARTY HOLSAPLE McCARTY, Knoxville	615 544 2000
ROOF DESIGN WORKS INC., Knoxville	615 584 6682
WEEKS & AMBROSE, Knoxville	615 546 8232
ALLEN & HOSHALL, Memphis	901 327 8222
ARCHEON, INC., Memphis	901 345 3244
ARCHITECTURAL RESOURCES GROUP, Memphis	901 725 0410
BOLOGNA & ASSOCIATES, Memphis	901 525 2557

AD BRADEN & ASSOCIATES, Memphis	901 761 0580	GOBBELL HAYS PARTNERS, INC., Nashville	615 254 8500
JOHN W. BURROUGHS, Memphis	901 682 6554	GRESHAM, SMITH, Nashville	615 385 3310
THE CROMWELL FIRM, Memphis	901 682 5180	BOB GWINN, Nashville	615 297 0410
THE CRUMP FIRM, Memphis	901 525 7744	HART FREELAND ROBERTS INC., Nashville	615 383 8652
DMS INC., Memphis	901 526 5080	HASTINGS ARCHITECTURE, Nashville	615 242 2113
A LOUIS ERTZ Memphis	901 767 2121	HAYES & ASSOCIATES, Nashville	615 383 8850
GREGORY GAY FAULKNER, Memphis	901 367 0742	HICKERSON FOWLKES, Nashville	615 329 4901
FLEMING ASSOCIATES, Memphis	901 767 3924	McFARLIN HUITT, Nashville	615 297 5422
HALL & WALLER & ASSOCIATES, Memphis	901 324 8887	McKISSACK & McKISSACK, Nashville	615 831 0278
ROY P HARROVER, Memphis	901 522 1406	ORR/HOUK, Nashville	615 383 4895
HILL-ARMOUR ASSOCIATED, Memphis	901 327 6188	MAXWELL OXFORD, Nashville	615 244 8170
HORRELL GROUP, Memphis	901 276 2721	REED & ASSOCIATES, Nashville	615 889 3120
JACKSON & BRONSON, Memphis	901 272 1617	R DOUGLAS ROBERTS, Nashville	615 385 0581
JONES MAH GASKILL RHODES, Memphis	901 526 9600	ROBERT B. RODGERS, Nashville	615 356 6900
LEE/ASKEY/NIXON/FERGUSON/WOLFE, Memphis	901 278 6868	JAMES F. SCALF & ASSOCIATES, Nashville	615 383 3668
LINDY AND ASSOCIATES, Memphis	901 767 6550	DONALD F. STEINBAUGH, Nashville	615 292 6502
LOONEY RICKS KISS, Memphis	901 521 1440	STREET AND STREET, Nashville	615 329 2564
MAHAN & SHAPPLEY ARCH., Memphis	901 767 9170	EARL SWENSSON, Nashville	615 329 9445
McFARLAND ASSOCIATES, Memphis	901 388 9490	KLINE SWINNEY, Nashville	615 255 1854
McGEHEE NICHOLSON BURKE, Memphis	901 683 7666	TUCK HINTON EVERTON, Nashville	615 320 1810
44 NATHAN EVANS POUNDERS & TAYLOR, Memphis	**901 525 5344**	YEARWOOD JONSON STANTON, Nashville	615 327 9300
JAMES L. OSTNER, Memphis	901 666 9409	MANUEL ZEITLIN, Nashville	615 385 0765
THE PICKERING FIRM, Memphis	901 726 0810	ADAMS CRAFT HERZ WALKER, Oak Ridge	615 482 4451
FRANK REPULT ARCHITECT, Memphis	901 683 7226	ALAN E. DILLOW, Sevierville	615 428 1250
JEAN PIERRE STOCKHEM, Memphis	901 726 6966	SAM H. McLEAN, Shelbyville	615 684 3822
TAYLOR GARDNER MONTGOMERY, Memphis	901 525 4446		
THORN HOWE STRATTON & STRONG, Memphis	901 767 1330	**T E X A S**	
JACK R. TUCKER, Memphis	901 523 0900	BOONE POPE WHEELER, Abilene	915 673 7334
CLIFTON WATSON, Memphis	901 767 4240	WOODLIEFF BROWN, Abilene	915 677 4405
JAMES WILLIAMSON/CARL AWSUMB, Memphis	901 526 2800	RICHARD BUZARD, Abilene	915 672 9012
WISEMAN/BLAND/FOSTER & O'BRIEN, Memphis	901 324 2104	CADCO ARCHITECTS, Abilene	915 695 6281
JOHNSON & BAILEY, Murfreesboro	615 890 4560	HENRY G. CASTLE, Abilene	915 672 5264
ADKISSON HARRISON & RICK, Nashville	615 298 9827	GRADY COZBY, Abilene	915 673 8291
ARCHITECTURE ASSOCIATES, Nashville	615 352 8107	ROBERT DURHAM, Abilene	915 692 7559
BARGE WAGGONER SUMNER & CANNON, Nashville	615 254 1500	MR NEWBERRY, Abilene	915 672 6454
WILLIAM BAYER, Nashville	615 259 4390	WEATHERL & WELCH, Abilene	915 673 6725
CLINTON E. BRUSH, Nashville	615 373 3014	MILLER TALLEY ASSOCIATES, Alice	512 664 5331
CORNERSTONE, Nashville	615 329 3989	WILLIAM A. MAY, Alvin	512 526 5744
SARA L. DENNIS, Nashville	615 269 4988	BOYETT ASSOCIATES, Amarillo	806 355 2081
THE EHRENKRANTZ GROUP & ECKSTUT, Nashville	615 242 2528	ENSIGN & TUNNELL, Amarillo	806 372 1671
FLOYD AND CORDIN, Nashville	615 327 2848	HANNON, DANIEL & DICKERSON, Amarillo	806 372 5144
JACK FREEMAN, Nashville	615 383 2144	RR INGERTON, Amarillo	806 355 9781

LAVIN ASSOCIATES, Amarillo	806 358 7069	THE BOWMAN GROUP, Austin	512 345 1138
CURTIS LESTER, Amarillo	806 835 0412	BROWN, JAMES & PFEIFFER, Austin	512 328 8580
LONGANECKER BLISS, Amarillo	806 372 3602	MARK CANADA, Austin	512 474 1906
MITCHELL SIMS, Amarillo	806 374 2341	JOHN L. CARLSCN, Austin	512 478 2598
JOHN NOTESTINE, Amarillo	806 355 7711	CARTER DESIGN, Austin	512 476 1812
PARGE ASSOCIATES, Amarillo	806 352 6312	LLOYD CATES, Austin	512 452 1082
SHIVER/MEGERT, Amarillo	806 372 5662	WILEY CHEATHAM, Austin	512 480 8020
WILSON DOCHE, Amarillo	806 373 3542	CHILES HOLLANDER, Austin	512 327 3397
LUTHER E. WOSSUM, Amarillo	806 374 1822	COFFEE, CRIER & SCHENCK, Austin	512 478 0741
HUCKABEE & DONHAM, Andrews	915 523 3450	COX/CROSLIN, Austin	512 346 8420
TERRY R. CUNNINGHAM, Arlington	817 649 8846	CROFT ASSOCIATES, Austin	512 346 0466
NORMAN W. DOUGLAS, Arlington	817 461 3257	DANZE AND DAVIS, Austin	512 343 0714
RB FERRIER, Arlington	817 469 8605	LES ELLASON & ASSOCIATES, Austin	512 258 6435
LYNN HOWERTON, Arlington	817 649 1543	MICHAEL DEAN ELLIOTT, Austin	512 478 4586
LEMONS & ASSOCIATES, Arlington	817 860 0400	EMERSON FEHR, Austin	512 346 2484
MALONE MAY ARCHITECTS, Arlington	817 465 4068	EUGENE GEORGE, Austin	512 467 9407
MIKUSEK MARSEE, Arlington	817 467 6171	GRAEBER, SIMMONS & COWAN, Austin	512 477 9417
JOHN R. MOORE, Arlington	817 795 3757	ROY GRAHAM, Austin	512 327 8020
ROBERT A. PATTERSON, Arlington	817 654 1616	LEE GROS, Austin	512 328 7202
PETRELLI ARCHITECT, Arlington	817 461 7330	BARRY M. HABER, Austin	512 345 8458
TAP ARCHITECTS, Arlington	817 640 4370	THOMAS H. HATCH, Austin	512 474 8548
THE VERKLER PARTNERSHIP, Arlington	817 265 0301	CLOVIS HEIMSATH, Austin	512 478 1621
VESTAL LOFTIS KALISTA, Arlington	817 277 9485	HINMAN MORTON HALFORD, Austin	512 480 9068
WHARTON & LAM, Arlington	817 265 1515	DAVID HOFFMAN, Austin	512 327 5885
CHARLES WILLIS, Arlington	817 261 1863	LM HOLDER III, Austin	512 328 0482
JOHN CHILES ALLEN, Austin	512 478 2109	ROBERT JACKSON, Austin	512 472 5132
AMERICAN DESIGN GROUP, Austin	512 328 3000	JESSEN INC., Austin	512 478 7437
ARCHITECTS OFFICE CORP., Austin	512 478 5555	KINNEY/KALER/CREWS, Austin	512 472 5572
ARCHITECTURE UNLIMITED, Austin	512 442 3888	DANIEL E. LEARY, Austin	512 478 5426
KEN ARTHUR II, Austin	512 477 1301	CHRIS LEWIS, Austin	512 474 8124
GARY ASHFORD, Austin	512 478 8262	EMILY LITTLE, Austin	512 477 3447
AUSTIN GROUP, Austin	512 343 6666	LTZ ARCHITECTS, Austin	512 343 6088
AUSTIN DESIGN ASSOCIATES, Austin	512 327 3709	WILLIAM S. MULLANE, Austin	512 835 9213
HERBERT BARNARD, Austin	512 258 5710	CHARTIER NEWTON & ASSOCIATES, Austin	512 478 7437
BARNES RUSSELL, Austin	512 476 7131	KENNETH M. NUHN, Austin	512 442 6392
BARROW AND STAHL, Austin	512 345 1170	JOHN V. NYFELER, Austin	512 478 3020
CHRISTINE BEALL, Austin	512 478 5873	O'CONNELL ROBERTSON GROBE, Austin	512 478 7286
MARVIN E. BECK, Austin	512 327 3050	PAGE SOUTHERLAND PAGE, Austin	512 472 6721
JOHN H. BERRY, Austin	512 258 6435	PARSHALL & ASSOCIATES, Austin	512 477 1696
BLACK/ATKINSON/VERNOOY, Austin	512 474 1632	A RAY PAYNE, Austin	512 343 7349
BLGY, INC., Austin	512 451 8281	PIERCE GOODWIN ALEXANDER, Austin	512 476 3568
BOWER DOWNING PARTNERSHIP, Austin	512 328 5320	KIRBY W. PERRY, Austin	512 478 2545

PFLUGER ASSOCIATES, Austin	512 476 4040
POLKINGHORN ARCHITECTS, Austin	512 477 9096
ROBERT B. PRINGLE, Austin	512 926 7288
RIO GROUP, Austin	512 440 8751
59 ROGERS & PERRY, Austin	**512 452 6744**
RTG PARTNERS INC., Austin	512 327 9296
SHEFELMAN & NIX, Austin	512 474 6262
DONALD R. SMALL, Austin	512 328 1902
ALAN Y. TANIGUCHI, Austin	512 474 7079
T.H.E. DESIGN, Austin	800 422 4843
VDW & ASSOCIATES, Austin	512 263 9332
VILLALVA, COTERA, KOLAR, Austin	512 474 6526
VOLZ & ASSOCIATES, Austin	512 476 0433
EDWARD B. WALLACE, Austin	512 452 0538
THE WHITE BUDD VAN NESS PARTNERSHIP, Austin	512 472 4912
PHIL WILLIAMS, Austin	512 477 2859
WILSON, STOELTJE, MARTIN, Austin	512 346 9472
WOLTER & ASSOCIATES, Austin	512 327 8453
ZAPALAC COMPANY, Austin	512 444 1809
HILL COUNTRY, Bandera	512 796 3198
WILLIAM T. BURGE, Baytown	713 420 3408
BUSCH HUTCHINSON & ASSOCIATES, Baytown	713 422 8213
DAVIS ASSOCIATES, Baytown	713 422 8393
THE LAMMERS PARTNERSHIP, Baytown	713 427 1737
MILTON BELL ASSOCIATES, Beaumont	409 838 5378
D REX GOODE, Beaumont	409 892 0963
CHARLES GOODELL, Beaumont	409 832 9757
GORDY & HUFFHINES, Beaumont	409 833 9136
GEORGE INGRAM ASSOCIATES, Beaumont	409 835 4546
STEINMAN/EIDE INC., Beaumont	409 833 4875
BROOKS & BROOKS, Bellaire	713 668 8650
RONALD FASH, Bellaire	713 668 5832
HIGHTOWER ALEXANDER, Bellaire	713 669 8005
THE RAPP PARTNERS, Bellaire	713 661 1751
REES ASSOCIATES, Bellaire	713 432 7337
W T REICHARDT, Bellaire	713 235 2523
MICHAEL J. STAPENHORST, Bellaire	713 666 0410
WATKINS CARTER HAMILTON, Bellaire	713 665 5665
GARY COMPANY, Big Spring	915 267 3151
JACK KENT, Blanco	512 833 5350
ASSOCIATED ARCHITECTS OF THE SOUTHWEST, Boerne	512 249 3639
HOLSTER & ASSOCIATES, Brazos	409 693 3179

GEORGE J. MANN, Brazos	409 845 1143
BOETTCHER & BOETTCHER, Brenham	409 836 0523
BALLI, GOMEZ, Brownsville	512 546 7146
DESIGN FIVE ARCHITECTS, Brownsville	512 546 9550
STANFORD C. KNOWLES, Brownsville	512 544 7959
ROBERT E. VELTEN, Brownsville	512 542 4586
GAYLE D. WILHITE, Brownsville	512 542 8547
CHARLIE BURRIS, Bryan	409 776 6433
JACK CUMPTON, Bryan	409 846 3771
GROUP 4 ARCHITECTS, Bryan	409 775 7472
MATTHEWS, CALLAN & ASSOCIATES, Bryan	713 846 7741
TORRANO/CAPORINA, Bryan	409 846 6389
EMMETT TRANT, Bryan	713 779 0769
ARCHITECTS DESIGN GROUP, Carrollton	214 960 1136
CALVERT AND COMPANY, Carrollton	214 446 0493
RAFAEL GARCIA, Carrollton	214 394 8126
LARRY J. HURLBUT, Carrollton	214 553 9555
MICHAEL PITTENGER, Carrollton	214 384 0555
MIKE BARNETT, Cedar Hill	214 341 1061
LEBOW McGEE, Cedar Hill	214 291 8852
TILLINGHAST/RANDALL, Clear Lake Shores	713 334 5535
HAMILTON & ASSOCIATES, Clute	409 265 6101
DON B. HILL, College Station	409 693 6163
CHARLES J. MULLER, Commerce	214 886 3350
JAMES C. PATTON, Commerce	214 886 7673
CHUCK ANASTOS, Corpus Christi	512 855 5881
BOGG CONSULTANTS, Corpus Christi	512 851 8825
BRIGHT AND DYKEMA, Corpus Christi	512 882 8171
COTTEN LANDRETH, Corpus Christi	512 884 3295
ENVIRONMENTAL DISCIPLINES, Corpus Christi	512 887 0701
KIPP RICHTER & ASSOCIATES, Corpus Christi	512 882 4466
MABREY DESIGNS, Corpus Christi	512 882 2922
McCORD & LORENZ, Corpus Christi	512 882 8275
OLSON ASSOCIATES, Corpus Christi	512 853 8721
ROOTS/FOSTER, Corpus Christi	512 855 6253
RUCKER & RUCKER, Corpus Christi	512 888 5756
TRIAN SERBU, Corpus Christi	512 949 7250
SMITH AND RUSSO, Corpus Christi	512 883 1984
MORGAN SPEAR ASSOCIATES, Corpus Christi	512 883 5588
WILLIAM STALTER, Corpus Christi	512 854 2665
AGUIREE ARCHITECTS, Dallas	214 788 1508
ALDREDGE & ASSOCIATES, Dallas	214 352 6210

NORMAN R. ALSTON, Dallas	214 324 1309
A.D. ANDERSON, Dallas	214 238 7561
ANPH ARCHITECTS, Dallas	214 369 9066
AR ARCHITECTS, Dallas	214 526 3790
ARCHITECTURAL DESIGNERS INC., Dallas	214 243 4030
ARCHITECTS CO., Dallas	214 770 2222
ARCHITECTURE PLUS, Dallas	214 343 3100
ARCHITEXAS, Dallas	214 748 4561
GEORGE BALLE, Dallas	214 368 1627
SAM S. BATES, Dallas	214 522 2323
MICHAEL BAUSCH, Dallas	214 528 5272
BENSON, HLAVATY ASSOCIATES, Dallas	214 220 4777
BERAN & SHELMIRE, Dallas	214 522 7980
BETHEL & WILLIAMS, Dallas	214 871 8774
BGR ARCHITECTS, Dallas	214 330 0431
GARY LYNN BLEVINS, Dallas	214 327 0108
BOOZIOTIS & CO., Dallas	214 350 5051
DAHL BRADEN PTM INC., Dallas	214 520 0077
BRANCH & TAYLOR, Dallas	214 770 2300
BRINKLEY, BRINKLEY & SARGENT, Dallas	214 960 9970
BROOKFIELD & LOWRY, Dallas	214 490 9020
BROWN REYNOLDS WATFORD, Dallas	214 528 8704
BURSON & COX, Dallas	214 871 8774
WILLIAM F. CALLEJO-BORGES, Dallas	214 747 4166
ROBERT H. CLARK, Dallas	214 361 9279
JIM COKER, Dallas	214 553 9555
COOK & HERMAN, Dallas	214 241 2507
CORGAN ASSOCIATES, Dallas	214 748 2000
BEN COREZ, Dallas	214 841 3190
CRAYCROFT ASSOCIATES, Dallas	214 522 6060
GARY M. CUNNINGHAM, Dallas	214 855 5272
DALLAS DESIGN GROUP, Dallas	214 358 3708
TOM F. DANCE, Dallas	214 960 6375
JAMES M. DAVIS, Dallas	214 528 1188
DEMAREST AND ASSOCIATES, Dallas	214 720 0188
DESIGN RESPONSE, Dallas	214 520 3500
DICKSON-WELLS, Dallas	214 871 0616
EPPS ARCHITECTS INC., Dallas	214 746 4346
F & S PARTNERS, Dallas	214 559 4851
FEDERICO ASSOCIATES, Dallas	214 238 1621
FLM ASSOCIATES, Dallas	214 871 0020
RICHARD F. FLOYD, Dallas	214 238 5670

FORRESTER ASSOCIATES, Dallas	214 871 0861
EDMUND GAZINSKI, Dallas	214 783 8100
GRAYSON GILL INC., Dallas	214 979 0355
GOOD FULTON FARRELL, Dallas	214 979 0028
GROMATSKY DUPREE, Dallas	214 991 9375
ALLAN WALTON HALL, Dallas	214 742 9525
HARPER, KEMPER, CLUTTS, Dallas	214 528 8644
RAYMOND HARRIS & ASSOCIATES, Dallas	214 749 0626
HASTINGS, TREVINO, Dallas	214 960 0644
HATFIELD HALCOMB ARCH., Dallas	214 931 9151
HEALTHCARD ENVIRONMENT DES., Dallas	214 820 2872
32/33 HELLMUTH, OBATA & KASSABAUM, INC., Dallas	**214 739 6688**
JACK HEMPHILL, Dallas	214 526 5185
HENNINGSON, DURHAM & RICHARDSON, Dallas	214 960 4000
WILLIAM H. HIDELL, Dallas	214 526 7791
WARDEN EVANS HILL, Dallas	214 386 6131
J. EDWARD HILLIARD, Dallas	214 348 9454
HKS, Dallas	214 969 5599
HMBH ARCHITECTS, Dallas	214 701 9000
HARRY C. HOOVER, Dallas	214 871 0380
HSJ ARCHITECTS, Dallas	214 528 9352
HARPER HUDDLESTON, Dallas	214 644 0606
GILBERTO IBARRA, Dallas	214 574 2573
IKEMIRE ARCHITECTS, Dallas	214 907 9900
INDEC TEXAS CORPORATION, Dallas	214 960 1102
34 INSPACE, Dallas	**214 428 8080**
BERNARD JOHNSON/TAYLOR HEWETT, Dallas	214 620 9262
JPJ ARCHITECTS, Dallas	214 987 8000
JRH ARCHITECTS, Dallas	214 979 0201
EDWARD JUST ASSOCIATES, Dallas	214 373 1239
MICHAEL D. KAESLER, Dallas	214 343 8388
WALTER E. KAESLER, Dallas	214 358 2886
KELLER ARCHITECT, Dallas	214 341 1601
KELLER BROWNING INC., Dallas	214 360 0091
KELMAN/DANIELS, Dallas	214 855 0815
KRAUSE & COLLIER ARCHITECTS, Dallas	214 631 3784
JAMES H. KRAUSE, Dallas	214 824 2400
LANDRY & LANDRY, Dallas	214 953 3137
LASSITER & ASSOCIATES, Dallas	214 343 8890
MAX LEVY, Dallas	214 368 2023
DAVID C. LUDWICK, Dallas	214 324 2013
PATE LUNDY, Dallas	214 526 2750

38/39 **MAGILL ARCHITECTS, INC., Dallas**	**214 343 1981**	
MANGAL, CRONAN, SHUFORD, Dallas	214 369 8300	
MAYSE & ASSOCIATES, Dallas	214 386 0338	
McCALL HARRIS, Dallas	214 526 1840	
McCUNE PARTNERS OF TEXAS, Dallas	214 248 2797	
MIDWAY, Dallas	214 934 3388	
MILLS & MILLS, Dallas	214 826 5501	
MLM ARCH. INC., Dallas	214 385 1900	
MORAN & ASSOCIATES, Dallas	214 871 8786	
MULLEN ARCHITECTS, Dallas	214 742 8949	
ROBERT J. MURRAY, Dallas	214 348 0305	
STUART C. MUT, Dallas	214 522 1819	
GARY GENE OLP, Dallas	214 422 0080	
OMNIPLAN, Dallas	214 742 1261	
J R OSBORNE, Dallas	214 235 6072	
PAGE SOUTHERLAND PAGE, Dallas	214 522 3902	
ALTON PARKER, Dallas	214 871 2101	
JOHN PERKINS, Dallas	214 742 2081	
PFANENSTIEL ARCHITECTS, Dallas	214 233 7823	
PHILLIPS SWAGER, Dallas	214 239 8827	
PICKLE & THOMAS ARCHITECTS, Dallas	214 233 5001	
PIERCE GOODWIN ALEXANDER, Dallas	214 750 1945	
RAYMOND POON, Dallas	214 497 5855	
MILTON POWELL, Dallas	214 526 2151	
PAUL J. RASH, Dallas	214 361 7175	
RAW SPACE FACILITIES, Dallas	214 681 0163	
REYNOLDS REYNOLDS WATFORD, Dallas	214 528 8704	
REYNOLDS & STONE ARCH., Dallas	214 638 0625	
JOHN DOUGLAS RICE, Dallas	214 339 9629	
RISEMAN ASSOCIATES, Dallas	214 361 9902	
MICHAEL E. ROGERS, Dallas	214 891 0811	
ROSSETTI ASSOCIATES, Dallas	214 522 7600	
60/61 **RTKL ASSOCIATES INC., Dallas**	**214 871 8877**	
62/63 **SASAKI ASSOCIATES, INC., Dallas**	**214 922 9380**	
SCH ARCHITECTS, Dallas	214 720 0390	
RANDALL SCOTT ARCHITECTS, Dallas	214 380 1234	
SDA ASSOCIATES, Dallas	214 934 9001	
SUSAN E. SEIFERT, Dallas	214 741 1261	
SELZER ASSOCIATES, Dallas	214 220 2121	
J. DAVID SHANKS, Dallas	214 931 9151	
SHEPHERD NELSON WHEELER, Dallas	214 691 2900	
SHWC, Dallas	214 373 9999	

GORDON SIBECK & ASSOCIATES, Dallas	214 871 0200
THE SKELTON GROUP, Dallas	214 361 7175
SMITH/EKBLAD, Dallas	214 742 4891
DONALD F. SOPRANZI, Dallas	214 701 9000
STB ARCHITECTS, Dallas	214 739 8080
SULLIVAN KEY MERRILL, Dallas	214 761 0505
SVI ARCHITECTS, Dallas	214 349 9505
TABAK DESIGN GROUP, Dallas	214 750 9604
PAUL A. TERRELL, Dallas	214 386 0797
THEATRE CONCEPTS, Dallas	214 386 0666
JOHN R. THOMPSON, Dallas	214 931 7150
THREE/ARCHITECTURE INC., Dallas	214 559 4080
J. STUART TODD, Dallas	214 720 1925
TOWN SCAPE ARCHITECTS, Dallas	214 324 8928
MICHAEL F. TWICHELL, Dallas	214 748 6461
THE VINCENT ASSOCIATION, Dallas	214 630 2902
STEVE WADDILL, Dallas	214 891 3233
WEETER & ASSOCIATES, Dallas	214 238 5950
WELCH & ASSOCIATES, Dallas	214 363 6966
WEST & HUMPHRIES, Dallas	214 363 9700
34 **WHITENER-ROHE, INC., Dallas**	**214 428 8080**
MICHAEL S. WILES, Dallas	214 931 5501
WILLIFORD ASSOCIATES, Dallas	214 343 0119
WILSON & ASSOCIATES, Dallas	214 521 6753
WOMACK HUMPHREYS ARCHITECTS, Dallas	214 770 2300
WOO, JAMES, HARWICK, PECK, Dallas	214 363 5687
WOODWARD & ASSOCIATES, Dallas	214 934 1122
WRIGHT RICH & ASSOCIATES, Dallas	214 750 0077
WSI ARCH., Dallas	214 458 9999
WTP INC., Dallas	214 871 0672
GUY FORD, Deer Park	713 479 4703
ARCHITECTURAL COLLECTIVE INC., Denton	817 387 4881
GARY JUREN, Denton	817 566 3316
MOUNT/MILLER, Denton	817 387 1659
TERRY F. BREWER, Duncanville	214 941 2442
EDWARD F. CUMMINGS, Duncanville	214 298 7053
ALVIDREZ ASSOCIATES, El Paso	915 533 8200
ANDERSON THACKER ASSOCIATES, El Paso	915 779 8432
BOOTH KEIRSEY MIJARES, El Paso	915 532 7023
BOYD AND ASSOCIATES, El Paso	915 545 1970
ARCHITECTS MORRIS BROWN, El Paso	915 593 8352
CARSON CONSULTANTS, El Paso	915 584 1104

DEGROOT AND ASSOCIATES, El Paso	915 533 4934	HARVEY YOUNGBLOOD, Fort Worth	817 332 2672
FISCHER CORDOVA PRESTIDGE, El Paso	915 544 2952	MICHAEL GAERTNER, Galveston	409 762 0500
FOSTER, HENRY, HENRY & THORPE, El Paso	915 544 2891	OLIVER ASSOCIATES, Galveston	409 762 2125
GARLAND & HILLES, El Paso	915 533 3937	THE RAPP PARTNERS, Galveston	409 765 5588
FOUTS GOMEZ, El Paso	915 544 4740	DAVID WATSON, Galveston	409 762 2018
JOE M. JAMES, El Paso	915 581 6853	LARSON DESIGN, Garland	214 742 6500
RICHARD A. LEDLOW, El Paso	915 592 4000	BYRON McCOLLUM, Garland	214 696 3775
McCORMICK, KUYKENDALL, McCOMBS, El Paso	915 779 3048	CBM DESIGN, Georgetown	512 837 0754
SAM T. MIDDLETON, El Paso	915 584 2915	VOELTER ASSOCIATES, Georgetown	512 863 9255
CARR/RAZLOZNIK, El Paso	915 532 2121	SEALE MAYFIELD, Grand Prairie	817 469 8271
GEORGE STATEN & ASSOCIATES, El Paso	915 544 7000	SMITH AND WARDER, Grand Prairie	214 262 1505
BYRON FOLSE, Euless	817 267 3596	3D/INTERNATIONAL, Houston	713 871 7000
ALEXANDER PATTERSON, Fort Worth	817 429 8256	ADAMS ARCHITECTURE, Houston	713 529 2592
STAN BAKER, Fort Worth	817 335 6983	KURT C. AICHLER, Houston	713 868 1136
THE ARCHITECTS BARNES ASSOCIATES, Fort Worth	817 731 8211	AMBROSE & McENANY, Houston	713 522 0815
BARRETT, DAFFIN & CARLAN, Fort Worth	817 731 0914	ARCHITECTURAL GROUP, Houston	713 522 4141
WARD BOGARD & ASSOCIATES, Fort Worth	817 625 7066	RAY BAILEY ARCHITECTS, Houston	713 524 2155
BOOTHE ARCHITECTS, Fort Worth	817 332 8998	ROYDEN S. BAIR, Houston	713 461 7350
ROBERT BRADLEY, Fort Worth	817 877 1987	KENNETH BALK & ASSOCIATES, Houston	713 931 9920
TONY DINICOLA, Fort Worth	817 281 7860	LARS BANG, Houston	713 977 1696
F R S DESIGN GROUP, Fort Worth	817 334 0556	BELL MANN CORP., Houston	713 880 9999
MARK GUNDERSON, Fort Worth	817 921 0583	THE BLACKSTONE PARTNERSHIP, Houston	713 681 5664
HAHNFELD ASSOCIATES, Fort Worth	817 335 1303	PM BOLTON ASSOCIATES, Houston	713 522 0827
HALBACH, DIETZ, Fort Worth	817 737 0725	JOEL BRAND ASSOCIATES, Houston	713 667 5928
V. AUBREY HALLUM, Fort Worth	817 870 2262	EDWIN S. BROADWELL, Houston	713 529 0159
TERRY M. HARDEN, Fort Worth	817 877 5171	BROOKS/COLLIER, Houston	713 520 9990
WILLIAM HERRINGTON, Fort Worth	817 332 3237	BROOKS ASSOCIATION, Houston	713 871 0667
KIRK VOICH & GIST, Fort Worth	817 335 4991	BUILDING SERVICES ASSOCIATES, Houston	713 529 5071
PAUL KOEPPE, Fort Worth	817 336 1981	THE BURFORD GROUP, Houston	713 789 4700
KOMATSU & ASSOCIATES, Fort Worth	817 332 1914	CANNADY, JACKSON & RYAN, Houston	713 526 8475
MAPLES ASSOCIATES, Fort Worth	817 336 0526	MITCHELL CARLSON, Houston	713 522 1054
NADER DESIGN GROUP, Fort Worth	817 336 9010	JIM CARTER & ASSOCIATES, Houston	713 468 1128
O'BRIEN PARTNERSHIP, Fort Worth	817 261 0595	CENTURY A-E, Houston	713 783 0055
PALMER ARCHITECTS, Fort Worth	817 926 8141	CHELSEA ARCHITECTS, Houston	713 960 0950
PARKER/CROSTON/LACKEY/BLAKE, Fort Worth	817 332 8464	CISNEROS/UNDERHILL, Houston	713 521 1405
RADY & ASSOCIATES, Fort Worth	817 335 6511	CLERKLEY GROUP, Houston	713 975 9196
DORLAND CAROL SHELTON, Fort Worth	817 737 5774	COMPENDIUM, Houston	713 526 2633
LEE STUART, Fort Worth	817 478 1497	CRS SIRRINE, Houston	713 552 2353
HAL J. SULLENBERGER, Fort Worth	817 642 5060	M T CRUMP, Houston	713 840 1702
VAUGHN ARCHITECTS PLUS, Fort Worth	817 732 5651	CTJ & D ARCHITECTS, Houston	713 977 6858
ARTHUR WEINMAN, Fort Worth	817 737 0977	DANSBY & MILLER, Houston	713 941 2751
YANDEL & HILLER, Fort Worth	817 335 3000	DCW ARCHITECTS, Houston	713 778 3044

REY DE LA REZA, Houston	713 868 3121	LOCKWOOD ANDREWS NEWMAN, Houston	713 266 6900
DIGIGRAPHIC, Houston	713 461 4240	GRAHAM B. LUHN, Houston	713 529 6969
JAMES D. DOUGLAS, Houston	713 890 0607	VICTOR LUNDY, Houston	713 522 4710
JOHN LAWLER DRYE, Houston	713 667 9813	TAPLEY LUNOW, Houston	713 522 2776
DUNAWAY & JONES, Houston	713 622 6910	MACKIE & KAMRATH, Houston	713 529 2696
ENVIRONMENT ASSOCIATES, Houston	713 528 0000	GERARD MANCUSO, Houston	713 870 1140
FALICK/KLEIN, Houston	713 782 9000	JOHN MARTIN ASSOCIATES, Houston	713 460 0493
RICHARD FITZGERALD, Houston	713 961 3221	MAURICE, WILKINS & JACKSON, Houston	713 622 4466
GABERT/ABUZALAF, Houston	713 527 0251	BRADEN McALLISTER, Houston	713 783 1747
GELSOMINO/JOHNSON, Houston	713 529 1050	MCCM ARCHITECTS, Houston	713 526 8600
HARRY GENDEL, Houston	713 622 2223	D. WAYNE McDONNELL, Houston	713 977 7685
GENSLER & ASSOCIATES, Houston	713 228 8050	BOVAY/McGINTY, Houston	713 439 0800
LORI GIEGER, Houston	713 783 3775	McGINTY PARTNERSHIP, Houston	713 880 2500
GOLDEN & JACKSON ARCHITECTS, Houston	713 526 5631	KAUFMAN MEEKS, Houston	713 789 1330
SHELBY GOODMAN, Houston	713 661 1653	JOHN MERK, Houston	713 666 9233
HALL ARCHITECTS, Houston	713 621 7581	MILLER WINDSOR, Houston	713 827 8884
KATHY HEARD DESIGN, Houston	713 522 2445	MOLINA & ASSOCIATES, Houston	713 782 8188
HEIGHTS VENTURE ARCHITECTS, Houston	713 869 1103	MORRIS ARCHITECTS, Houston	713 622 1180
HERMES REED HINDMAN, Houston	713 785 3644	BONHAM NEMETI, Houston	713 952 0242
HOOVER & FURR, Houston	713 871 7069	WO NEUHAUS, Houston	713 523 5107
JOHN F. HOUCHINS, Houston	713 522 6094	PAGE SOUTHERLAND PAGE, Houston	713 974 5420
CHARLES HUBBARD, Houston	713 880 1330	DMP & ASSOCIATES, INC., Houston	713 785 6980
ROBERT HUSMANN, Houston	713 664 6658	PBR ARCHITECTS, Houston	713 965 0608
HC HWANG, Houston	713 622 6888	PHILO ARCHITECTS, Houston	713 622 4114
INDEX INC., Houston	713 977 2594	PIERCE, GOODWIN, ALEXANDER, Houston	713 977 5777
IRVINE ASSOCIATES, Houston	713 840 1880	R & A ARCHITECTS, Houston	713 981 7315
BERNARD JOHNSON INC., Houston	713 622 1400	MRW ARCHITECTS, Houston	713 621 1651
ERIC M. JONES, Houston	713 792 2232	EDWARD F. ROGERS, Houston	713 789 3478
KAUFMAN MEEKS INC., Houston	713 558 8787	LLEWELYN, DAVIES, SAHNI, Houston	713 850 1500
MICHAEL KEENE ARCHITECTS, Houston	713 623 6468	OAD, Houston	713 526 2633
KEEPER COMPANY, Houston	713 623 6446	SEEBERGER & ASSOCIATES, Houston	713 682 1161
VIRGINIA KELSEY, Houston	713 871 7361	CARRIE GLASSMAN SHOEMAKE, Houston	713 521 3353
KENDALL/HEATON, Houston	713 877 1192	SHWC, INC., Houston	713 875 6666
RL KIRKENDALL, Houston	713 524 0525	SIKES/JENNINGS/KELLY/BREWER, Houston	713 781 8600
KIRKSEY MEYERS, Houston	713 850 9600	ARCHITECTURE PLUS, Houston	713 496 6778
KURTH, BROWN & ASSOCIATES, Houston	713 521 2019	SOURCE ARCHITECTS, INC., Houston	713 578 9567
LAN ARCHITECTS, Houston	713 266 6900	SPENCER HEROLZ ARCH., Houston	713 522 1666
CHARLES A. LANCLOS, Houston	713 465 1464	THE STEINBERG COLLABORATIVE, Houston	713 526 2676
LANGWITH, WILSON, KING, Houston	713 621 1890	TAFT ARCHITECTS, Houston	713 522 2988
LEIFESTE/BELANGER, Houston	713 782 0081	TAPLEY/LUNOW ARCHS., Houston	713 465 4679
LEVY ASSOCIATES, Houston	713 528 2912	TEAM HOU INC., Houston	713 524 4824
JANITO LO & ASSOCIATES, Houston	713 621 8821	TRACY & WEBB, Houston	713 467 1754

R GREGORY TURNER, Houston	713 497 1040	
UNICA DESIGN INC., Houston	713 869 0813	
WATKINS CARTER HAMILTON, Houston	713 665 5665	
THE WHITE BUDD VAN NESS PARTNERSHIP, Houston	713 622 3910	
O RUSSELL WORLEY, Houston	713 526 2025	
WRJA CORPORATION, Houston	713 524 9114	
ZIEGLER COOPER INC., Houston	713 654 0000	
JOHN B. MONTGOMERY, Huntsville	713 460 9891	
ROBERT S. ALLAN, Irving	214 637 6004	
RICHARD J. BRYANT, Irving	214 253 0496	
BURLESON ASSOCIATES, Irving	214 550 7447	
CHAKOS ZENTNER MARCUM, Irving	214 830 6167	
16 CHRIS CONSULTANTS, INC., Irving	**214 253 3583**	
ELAM ASSOCIATES, Irving	214 550 1355	
HAMILL & McKINNEY, Irving	214 580 0461	
JERRY Q. JEFFERY, Irving	214 790 2300	
REES ASSOCIATES, Irving	214 630 7337	
JOHN HENDERSON, Kerrville	512 257 8550	
ARCHITECTS PLUS, Laredo	512 723 2222	
CAVAZOS & ASSOCIATES, Laredo	512 724 8123	
TURNER HICKEY & ASSOCIATES, Laredo	512 722 8186	
ASHLEY HUMPHRIES, Laredo	512 723 2939	
ALLEN/BUIE PARTNERSHIP, Longview	214 753 5502	
BRATZ THACKER, Longview	214 216 3771	
HAROLD DETEAU, Longview	214 753 1082	
MALLOY & BRESIE, Longview	214 758 4478	
SINGLETON ROBINETT, Longview	214 297 7777	
WALSH/MORRIS, Longview	214 758 6200	
AC ASSOCIATES, Lubbock	806 747 0168	
ADLING ASSOCIATES, Lubbock	806 795 5908	
BGR ARCHITECTS, Lubbock	806 747 3881	
BILL COX, Lubbock	806 762 1226	
MARTIN ARCHITECTURE, Lubbock	806 747 3517	
JOE D. McKAY, Lubbock	806 795 7146	
MWM ARCHITECTS, Lubbock	806 745 7707	
SUNWEST CONSTRUCTION, Lubbock	806 797 2775	
MORGAN, O'NEAL, HILL & SUTTON, Lufkin	409 632 3353	
ASHLEY HUMPHRIES, McAllen	512 687 5254	
MWM, Midland	915 682 4482	
JAMES R. RHOTENBERRY JR., Midland	915 682 1252	
ALTON YOWELL, Midland	915 682 6582	
FIELDS & ASSOCIATES, Odessa	915 367 4829	

JOHNSON SEEFELDT, Odessa	915 362 6565
DENNEY ARCHITECTS, Paris	214 785 4318
JL BRANTLEY, Plano	214 442 5601
ARTHUR SCHWARTZ, Plano	214 881 0647
SHIVE HATTERY, Plano	214 578 8361
CHARLES BIRKHEAD, Richardson	214 644 1977
BROWN BROWN & ASSOCIATES, Richardson	214 235 8379
RICHARD FERRARA, Richardson	214 470 0171
RF HODGKINSON, Richardson	214 231 0716
OVERLAND PARTNERSHIP, San Antonio	512 829 7003
CRAIG ALLEN, San Antonio	512 824 3446
ROBERT ARBURN, San Antonio	512 349 5184
ARCHITECT INC., San Antonio	512 828 8412
BENDER ASSOCIATES, San Antonio	512 696 4116
THE BENHAM GROUP, San Antonio	512 491 9500
KEN BENTLEY, San Antonio	512 732 1169
PETER CALLINS & ASSOCIATES, San Antonio	512 824 1435
CAMPOS & HAZELWOOD, San Antonio	512 225 6504
CHUMNEY & ASSOCIATES, San Antonio	512 271 9400
DURAND-HOLLIS, San Antonio	512 696 1810
FORD POWELL & CARSON, San Antonio	512 226 1246
HAYWOOD JORDAN McCOWAN, San Antonio	512 337 5250
HESSON ANDREWS SOTOMAYOR, San Antonio	512 820 0888
JDM, San Antonio	512 340 4923
JOHNSON DEMPSEY, San Antonio	512 828 6251
JONES & KELL, San Antonio	512 349 1163
KINNISON & ASSOCIATES, San Antonio	512 732 2248
LAKE/FLATO, San Antonio	512 227 3335
MARMON BARCLAY SOUTER FOSTER, San Antonio	512 223 9492
McCALL & ASSOCIATES, San Antonio	512 344 9035
MENDOZA & ASSOCIATES, San Antonio	512 828 4958
MIDDLEMAN & DE LA GARZA, San Antonio	512 342 3197
MORKOVSKY & ASSOCIATES, San Antonio	512 341 5565
NOONAN, DOCKERY, NOONAN & ROGERS, San Antonio	512 226 0203
O'NEILL CONRAD OPPELT, San Antonio	512 829 1737
PEMBERTON HAUGH, San Antonio	512 534 7462
ANDREW PEREZ, San Antonio	512 227 1900
CHARLES H. RANDALL, San Antonio	512 822 7441
REGNIER, VALDEZ & ASSOCIATES, San Antonio	512 532 3212
REHLER VAUGHN BEATY & KOONE, San Antonio	512 828 9090
REITZER CRUZ ARCHITECTS, San Antonio	512 736 6605
HUMBERTO SALDANA, San Antonio	512 227 4040

SPEEGLE & ASSOCIATES, San Antonio	512 228 9921
LK TRAVIS, San Antonio	512 224 4041
EMMIT R. TUGGLE, San Antonio	512 222 0194
PARKS, HAAS & ASSOCIATES, San Marcos	512 353 3010
ADAMS GRABLE & KRAUS, Schertz	512 340 5151
LOGSDON & VOELTER, Temple	817 778 3221
W. GLENN RUCKER, Temple	817 778 0877
ATKINS PARTNERSHIP, Terrell	214 932 4265
MICHAEL D. BARHAM, Tyler	214 561 8110
ROBERT Y. BROWN, Tyler	214 561 7281
BURCH ASSOCIATES, Tyler	214 593 5605
LEL L. MEDFORD, Tyler	214 593 7997
SINCLAIR AND WRIGHT, Tyler	214 595 2656
WILCOX ASSOCIATES, Tyler	214 592 1052
BENNETT CARNAHAN HEARN & THOMAS, Waco	817 755 7955
DUDLEY BAILEY JEZEK & ROSE, Waco	817 776 8380
RASO GREAVES ARCHITECTURE, Waco	817 753 4753
ROBERT SCHRAPLAU, Wylie	214 442 5059

U.S. VIRGIN ISLANDS

LAMBERT R. PIERCE & ASSOCIATES, Frederiksted	809 772 2525
FRANK BLAYDON & ASSOCIATES, St. Croix	809 773 1109
CAPE, PC, DA WILLIAMS, St. Croix	809 775 7450
ISLAND ARCHITECTS, St. John	809 776 6700
C. WILLIAM RICH ARCHITECT, St. John	809 776 7769
AMBIENT GROUP, St. Thomas	809 776 8386
DEJONGH ASSOCIATES, St. Thomas	809 774 8035
JOHN GARFIELD & ASSOCIATES, St. Thomas	809 774 0350
KRAMER ASSOCIATES, St. Thomas	809 775 5232
DEAN W. OLSON, St. Thomas	809 776 0310
ALBERT SIGAL AND ASSOCIATES, St. Thomas	809 774 4350
HERMAN F. TERWEE & ASSOCIATES, St. Thomas	809 775 6531
78/79 **DOUGLAS WHITE ARCHITECT, St. Thomas**	**809 775 7843**

VENEZUELA

58 **RIVAS/KERDEL & DIAS/AIDOS C.A., Caracas**	**32.90.11**